LITERATURE
FOR ENGLISH

ADVANCED TWO

Burton Goodman

McGraw Hill — Wright Group

Series Editor: Anne Petti Smith
Executive Editor: Linda Kwil
Creative Director: Michael E. Kelly
Marketing Manager: Thomas Dare
Production Manager: Genevieve Kelley

 Wright Group

Send all inquiries to:

Wright Group/McGraw-Hill
One Prudential Plaza
130 E. Randolph Ave. Suite 400
Chicago, IL 60601

ISBN: 0-07-256525-X

Printed in the United States of America.

2 3 4 5 6 7 8 9 10 QPD 08 07 06 05

The **McGraw·Hill** Companies

CONTENTS

Acknowledgments

Acknowledgment is gratefully made to the following publishers, authors, and agents for permission to reprint these works. Adaptations and/or abridgements are by Burton Goodman. Retellings of "After Twenty Years," "The Stove," and "An Occurrence at Owl Creek Bridge," are by Burton Goodman. All rights reserved.

"The Teacher." Reprinted with the permission of Atheneum Books for Young Readers, an imprint of Simon & Schuster Children's Publishing Division, from *Where the Flame Trees Bloom* by Alma Flor Ada. Text copyright © 1994 Alma Flor Ada.

"The Tiger." From *Famous Chinese Short Stories* by Lin Yutang. All attempts have been made to locate the copyright holder.

"Early Autumn" from *Short Stories* by Langston Hughes. Copyright © 1996 by Ramona Bass and Arnold Rampersad. Reprinted by permission of Hill & Wang, a division of Farrar, Straus and Giroux, LLC.

"The City" from *Collected Poems of Langston Hughes* by Langston Hughes. Copyright © 1994 by The Estate of Langston Hughes. Used by permission of Alfred A. Knopf, a division of Random House, Inc.

"Lonely House" by Langston Hughes. All attempts have been made to locate the copyright holder.

"Declaration" from *Collected Poems of Langston Hughes* by Langston Hughes. Copyright © 1994 by The Estate of Langston Hughes. Used by permission of Alfred A. Knopf, a division of Random House, Inc.

"Dreams" from *Collected Poems of Langston Hughes* by Langston Hughes. Copyright © 1994 by The Estate of Langston Hughes. Used by permission of Alfred A. Knopf, a division of Random House, Inc.

"Ta-Na-E-Ka" by Mary Whitebird. From Scholastic Magazine. Reprinted by permission of Scholastic Inc.

"Grandfather" by James K. Cazalas. All attempts have been made to locate the copyright holder.

"The Circuit" by Francisco Jiménez. Copyright Arizona Board of Regents. Reprinted by permission of Arizona Board of Regents.

"A Secret for Two" by Quentin Reynolds. All attempts have been made to locate the copyright holder.

"Moco Limping" by David Nava Monreal from *Sights and Songs of Aztlán* (Bakersfield: Universal Press, 1975), pp. 62-3. By permission of F.E. Alibi, ed.

TO THE TEACHER

ABOUT THE *LITERATURE FOR ENGLISH* PROGRAM

Literature for English is a literature-based skills program designed to help readers improve their basic English skills.

Each book in the series contains outstanding stories by famous writers. The language in the stories is controlled so that they can be easily understood by students. Depending on the level, the stories are divided into a number of short, illustrated sections to assist the reader in understanding the selection. Many of the chapters in the Advanced Levels contain theme-related stories and poems.

A pre-reading section entitled **GETTING READY TO READ** introduces each story in this book. The component parts, **The Story and You, Learning About Literature,** and **Looking Ahead,** provide high-interest material to motivate the learner to read the story that follows. This section also offers important information about elements of literature.

Each story is followed by a comprehensive four-part skills check that is specially developed to meet the needs of LEP readers and is consistent with the general scope and sequence for ESL curricula.

The skills check provides a wide variety of hands-on practice in reading, writing, speaking, and listening. It includes the following exercises:

CHECK YOUR READING Ten self-scoring multiple-choice questions review reading comprehension, vocabulary, and idioms in the story just read. A Score Chart at the end of the book enables readers to enter their scores and see their results.

UNDERSTANDING THE STORY Varied exercises use directed writing activities for mastery of reading comprehension, sentence structure, verbs, parts of speech, writing, and punctuation. Hints to help the reader improve spelling and grammar are offered throughout.

STUDYING THE STORY Post-reading activities provide opportunities for students to work together to improve their listening, speaking, and writing skills. Specific as well as open-ended writing assignments and exercises appear in the sections **Studying the Story** and in the final section, **THINKING ABOUT LITERATURE**. Readers also complete a graphic organizer for each selection.

Literary elements explored in this series include character, plot, setting, conflict, and theme, as well as genre, such as the folktale, science fiction, and autobiography. In addition, this book contains features designed to teach and reinforce critical reading skills, such as making predictions, drawing conclusions, and reaching a decision by making inferences.

The vocabulary for each book in the series is drawn primarily from core word lists for beginning, intermediate, and advanced level students. Skills development is progressive, although it is possible to alter the sequence for intermediate and advanced level readers.

It should be noted that the Beginning book and Intermediate books use line reference numbers in the margins of the stories. These are extremely useful not only in helping the reader locate specific answers, but also in providing easy reference for reinforcement and review. The Beginning and Intermediate books also contain certain words and phrases printed in **boldfaced** type. This identifies the vocabulary and idioms that readers are tested on in the multiple-choice section following each chapter.

The Teacher's Guide provides the Answer Key for scoring **CHECK YOUR READING**, as well as suggested answers for the exercises in **UNDERSTANDING THE STORY**.

I appreciate the contributions of the many teachers, students, administrators, and ESL coordinators who offered assistance in the development of the *Literature for English* series. For their valuable suggestions, I am grateful.

The program's fine literature, attractive format, and positive approach should encourage the reader to enjoy literature and to improve their English.

Burton Goodman

SCOPE & SEQUENCE

Story	Reading Skills	Literary Elements	Grammar Structures
Unit 1: **The Teacher** *page 1*	■ summarizing	■ main character ■ characterization ■ character development	■ synonyms ■ word families
Unit 2: **The Tiger** *page 19*	■ summarizing ■ description	■ plot	■ simple and compound sentences ■ using coordinating conjunctions ■ synonyms ■ antonyms
Unit 3: After **Twenty Years** *page 41*	■ making inferences ■ comparison & contrast ■ thinking critically	■ surprise ending ■ dialogue	■ synonyms ■ antonyms
Unit 4: **The Stove** *page 59*	■ distinguishing fact from opinion	■ conflict ■ character ■ plot ■ simile	■ using connectives ■ synonyms
Unit 5: **Early Autumn** *page 83*	■ making inferences ■ drawing conclusions ■ making predictions ■ sequencing	■ conflict ■ inner conflict ■ *poetry:* stanzas ■ simile ■ metaphor	■ punctuation ■ synonyms ■ word families
Unit 6: An **Occurrence at** **Owl Creek Bridge** *page 105*	■ making predictions ■ thinking critically ■ description	■ setting ■ character traits ■ flashback	■ combining sentences ■ using subordinating conjunctions ■ synonyms
Unit 7: **Ta-Na-E-Ka** *page 125*	■ comparison & contrast	■ narrator ■ character ■ character development ■ plot	■ combining sentences ■ adjective clauses ■ subordinate clauses ■ relative pronouns ■ synonyms
Unit 8: **The Circuit** *page 147*	■ drawing conclusions ■ thinking critically ■ sequencing	■ *style:* autobiography ■ setting ■ main character	■ complex sentences ■ using subordinating conjunctions ■ synonyms
Unit 9: A **Secret for Two** *page 167*	■ using story clues	■ theme ■ setting ■ foreshadowing	■ direct quotations ■ reported speech ■ synonyms

THE TEACHER

BY ALMA FLOR ADA

GETTING READY TO READ

1. The Story and You

In this story, you will meet Lola, a teacher who suggests that we have "responsibility as human beings for those around us." Do you agree or disagree with Lola that people have some responsibility for others? If so, how much? Does it depend on the situation? Perhaps you believe that people should just "mind their own business"? What do you think? Explain your point of view.

2. Learning About Literature

In literature, there are various ways that an author can show what a character is like. The author can describe what a character looks like. The author can tell what a character thinks about and says. The author can also describe a character's actions. All of these **characterize** the people in a story. As you read "The Teacher," notice the ways in which the author characterizes Lola. Sometimes, during the course of a story, a character changes. This is known as **character development**. Look for an example of character development in "The Teacher."

3. Looking Ahead

Look at the illustration on the left. Does the story take place in the city or in the country? Does it take place indoors or outside? What do you think the weather is like? Look at the expression on the face of the man near the tree. How do you think he feels? Which character is the teacher? How do you know? Read on to see if you are right.

1

THE TEACHER

BY ALMA FLOR ADA

Life was her classroom . . .

My mother's mother, my grandmother Dolores, was known as Lola. She filled my early years with outdoor adventures, fun, and fascinating stories. The deeds of the Greek gods and goddesses, the heroic acts of the Cuban patriots, were as immediate to me as her everyday life at the two schools where she was principal: an elementary public school during the day and a school for working women in the evenings.

It is not surprising that there are many stories in our family about this woman who was both an intellectual and a practical person, who cut her hair and shortened her skirts before any other woman in our town, who created a literary journal, set up schools, awakened a great passion in the poet who married her, and brought up five children as well as several nieces and nephews while directing her own schools and farm.

One of my favorite stories about her was told to me at various times by my mother and by my aunts Mireya and Virginia, since all three of them were present when the events took place. Unlike many other family stories, which are often changed or embellished depending on the teller, I have always heard this story told exactly the same way. Perhaps that is because the story itself is too powerful to be embellished, or because the events impressed themselves so vividly upon the memories of those present.

My grandmother Lola loved to teach outdoors. The slightest reason would serve to take the whole class out under the trees to conduct her lessons there. This particular story took place during one of those outdoor lessons, at a time when she and her husband, my grandfather Medardo, ran a boarding school on the hacienda[1] she had inherited from her father and where later I would be born.

Surrounded by her pupils, including three of her own daughters, my grandmother was conducting a grammar lesson. Suddenly she interrupted herself. "Why is it," she asked her students, "that we don't often speak about the things that are truly important? About our responsibility as human beings for those around us? Do we really know their feelings, their needs? And yet we could all do so much for each other. . . ."

The students were silent, fascinated. They knew their teacher sometimes strayed[2] from the topic of the lesson in order to share with them her own reflections. And they also knew that those were some of her most important lessons. At times she could be funny and witty. Other times, she would touch their hearts. And so they listened.

"Look," continued my grandmother, as she pointed to the road that bordered the farm. There the students saw a solitary man walking. "Look at that old man. He is walking by us. In a few minutes he will be gone forever, and we will never have known who he is, where he is going, what may be important in his life."

The students watched the man, who by then was quite close. He was very thin, and a coarse guayabera[3] hung loosely over his bent frame. His face, in the shade of a straw hat, was tired and wrinkled.

"Well," said my grandmother, "do we let him go away, forever unknown, or do you want to ask him if there is anything we can do for him?"

The students looked at one another. Finally one girl said, "Shall I ask him?" As my grandmother nodded, the girl got up and walked toward the road. A few of the other students followed her, my

---

1. *hacienda*: a large ranch

2. *strayed*: wandered away

3. *guayabera*: a loose-fitting shirt

mother and my aunts among them.

Upon seeing them approach, the man stopped. "We would like to know who you are, and where you are going," said the student. "Is there anything we can do for you?" added my aunt Mireya.

The man was completely shocked. "But, who are *you*?" was all he could reply.

The girls then explained how their questions had come about. The old man looked at them. He told them that he had no one to be with, that he had come a long distance hoping to find some distant relatives, but had been unable to locate them. "I'm nothing but an old man," he concluded, "looking for a place to lie down and die. As a matter of fact, I was heading toward that large *ceiba*." He pointed to a large tree growing by the road not too far away. "I thought I'd lie down in its shade to wait for my death."

"Please don't leave" was all the girls could say. They rushed back to tell their teacher what they had learned from the old man, that he truly intended to just lie down and die.

"What do you think can be done?" my grandmother asked. The boys and girls came up with ideas: The old man could go to an old folks' home. Maybe he should be taken to the hospital, or perhaps the police would know what to do. . . . "Is that what you would like to happen, if it were you?" my grandmother asked.

Instead, the children took the man into the house. He was given a room. The students made the bed and cooked him some food. A doctor determined that there was nothing wrong with him except exhaustion and malnutrition. It took him several days to recuperate, but soon he was up and about. He lived on with the family for many years, until one morning he was found to have died peacefully in his sleep. During all those years, he helped in the garden, fed the hens, or often sat on the back porch, whistling softly. But there was nothing he liked better than to sit in the back of the classroom or out under the trees and listen to my grandmother teach.

Meet the Author

Alma Flor Ada (born 1938) grew up in Cuba and lived in Spain and Peru before moving to California where she now lives. She is the author of many popular children's books and mystery novels for young adults. Ada is a professor of Multicultural Education at the University of San Francisco. She is also president of the International Association for Children's Literature in Spanish and Portuguese. "The Teacher" appears in one of her best-known books, *Where the Flame Trees Bloom*. Her other works include *The Wall's Dwarf and Other Tales* and *The Ladybug's Dots and Other Stories*.

CHECK YOUR READING

Put an **X** in the box next to the correct answer.

<table>
<tr><td colspan="2">How many questions did you answer correctly? Circle your score. Then fill in your score on the Score Chart on page 184.</td></tr>
<tr><td>Number Correct</td><td>Score</td></tr>
<tr><td>1</td><td>10</td></tr>
<tr><td>2</td><td>20</td></tr>
<tr><td>3</td><td>30</td></tr>
<tr><td>4</td><td>40</td></tr>
<tr><td>5</td><td>50</td></tr>
<tr><td>6</td><td>60</td></tr>
<tr><td>7</td><td>70</td></tr>
<tr><td>8</td><td>80</td></tr>
<tr><td>9</td><td>90</td></tr>
<tr><td>10</td><td>100</td></tr>
</table>

Reading Comprehension

1. The author's grandmother was
- ☐ **a.** a doctor.
- ☐ **b.** a lawyer.
- ☐ **c.** a principal.

2. Grandmother Lola loved to
- ☐ **a.** teach outdoors.
- ☐ **b.** watch television.
- ☐ **c.** play baseball and other sports.

3. Which expression best describes the old man who was walking nearby?
- ☐ **a.** young and vigorous
- ☐ **b.** old and thin
- ☐ **c.** smiling and joyful

4. The man said that he was looking for
- ☐ **a.** his son.
- ☐ **b.** his wife.
- ☐ **c.** a place to die.

5. Where did the children take the man?
- ☐ **a.** into the house
- ☐ **b.** to a hospital
- ☐ **c.** to the police

6. What did the man like to do most?
- ☐ **a.** work in the garden
- ☐ **b.** feed the hens
- ☐ **c.** listen to Lola teach

Vocabulary

7. The students saw nothing but a solitary man walking along a road. The word *solitary* means
- ☐ **a.** alone.
- ☐ **b.** heavy.
- ☐ **c.** smart.

8. The man had walked for a long time and was suffering from exhaustion. Someone who is suffering from *exhaustion* is
- ☐ **a.** out of work.
- ☐ **b.** very tired.
- ☐ **c.** very poor.

9. The teacher liked to share her reflections with the students. As used here, the word *reflections* means
- ☐ **a.** food.
- ☐ **b.** thoughts.
- ☐ **c.** faces in a mirror.

Idioms

10. Grandmother Lola brought up five children and several nieces and nephews. The idiom *brought up* means
- ☐ **a.** pulled along.
- ☐ **b.** sent to many schools.
- ☐ **c.** watched over and helped grow.

UNDERSTANDING THE STORY

Exercise A ~ Checking Comprehension

Answer each question by writing a complete sentence. Be sure your sentences are grammatically correct. You may look back at the story.

1. Where did Grandmother Lola work as a principal during the day?

_____

2. Where did she work as a principal in the evenings?

_____

3. Describe the face of the old man who was walking by.

_____

4. What did a student ask the man?

_____

5. Who was the man looking for?

_____

6. What was the man planning to do?

_____

7. What did the doctor say about the man?

_____

8. How long did the man live with the family?

_____

9. How did the man help the family?

_____

10. What did the man like to do most?

_____

Exercise B ~ Adding Vocabulary

In the box are 10 words from the story. Complete each sentence by adding the correct word. The first one has been done for you.

wrinkled	concluded	patriots	malnutrition	heroic
responsibility	inherited	slightest	intellectual	conducting

1. Since Grandmother Lola's stories often told of _heroic_ acts, the children enjoyed the tales she told.

2. She sometimes taught at a ranch that she had

_____ from her father.

3. Grandmother Lola believed that human beings should accept

_____ for each other.

4. She loved to teach outdoors. Whenever she had the

_____ reason, she took the class outside.

5. Grandmother Lola read many books and wrote stories and poems. She

was a very _____ person.

6. The children heard tales about the courage of the Cuban

_____.

7. One afternoon, Grandmother Lola was _____ a lesson in grammar.

8. They saw a man whose face was tired and _____.

9. Since he was suffering from _____, they gave him some food.

10. "I am nothing but an old man," he _____.

Exercise C ~ Writing Sentences from Random Notes
Part A

Write a complete sentence for each group of words. Add capital letters, periods, and the appropriate words. Write the completed sentences on the lines. You may look back at the story. The first one has been done for you.

1. Grandmother Lola teaching a class

One day Grandmother Lola was teaching a class outdoors.

2. an old man walking by

3. asked the students if they wanted

4. student asked the man

5. looking for a place to die

6. took the old man into the house and

_____

_____

_____

7. recovered and lived happily

_____

_____

_____

Part B

Now **summarize** the story in a paragraph by using the sentences you wrote.
The first sentence of the paragraph appears below.

One day Grandmother Lola was teaching a
class outdoors.

_____

_____

_____

_____

_____

_____

_____

_____

_____

_____

_____

Exercise D ~ Finding Synonyms

Read the sentence. Then select the **synonym** (the word most similar in meaning) for the word in capital letters. Put an **X** in the box next to the correct answer. Each capitalized word appears in the story. The first one has been done for you.

1. Grandmother Lola told the children about the deeds of the Greek gods and goddesses.

   DEEDS
   - ☒ **a.** action
   - ☐ **b.** problems
   - ☐ **c.** homes

2. They never forgot the story; they remembered it vividly.

   VIVIDLY
   - ☐ **a.** poorly
   - ☐ **b.** clearly
   - ☐ **c.** happily

3. Lola was often serious, but she could be funny and witty.

   WITTY
   - ☐ **a.** sad
   - ☐ **b.** scared
   - ☐ **c.** amusing

4. They learned of the heroic acts of people who loved their country.

   HEROIC
   - ☐ **a.** easy
   - ☐ **b.** lucky
   - ☐ **c.** brave

5. Their teacher sometimes strayed from the lesson she was teaching.

   STRAYED
   - ☐ **a.** wandered
   - ☐ **b.** wrote
   - ☐ **c.** forgot

6. The topic of the lesson was grammar that day.

   TOPIC
   - ☐ **a.** test
   - ☐ **b.** subject
   - ☐ **c.** beginning

7. The old man said that he intended to lie down and die.

   INTENDED
   - ☐ **a.** planned
   - ☐ **b.** asked
   - ☐ **c.** rushed

8. He had been looking for some relatives, but he was unable to locate them.

   LOCATE
   - ☐ **a.** write
   - ☐ **b.** help
   - ☐ **c.** find

9. A doctor determined that the man needed food and rest.

   DETERMINED
   - ☐ **a.** hoped
   - ☐ **b.** decided
   - ☐ **c.** remembered

10. It took the man several days to recuperate, but soon he was walking around.

    RECUPERATE
    - ☐ **a.** recover
    - ☐ **b.** obey
    - ☐ **c.** wash

Exercise E ~ Word Families

Fill in the blanks by writing the correct word from each family of words. Use each word once. The first one has been done for you.

fascinate	fascinates	fascinated	fascinating	fascination

1. The author's grandmother was famous for telling _fascinating_ stories.

2. The students were silent and listened, _____, to what their teacher was saying.

3. Do the tales of the Greek gods and goddesses _____ you?

4. Lola's amazing energy and wide range of interests were a source of

   _____ to everyone who knew her.

5. I will take the book out of the library because the subject

   _____ me.

create	creating	creative	creation	creativity

6. Lola was a _____ person , who entertained her grandchildren with exciting stories she made up.

7. She was famous for _____ a literary journal.

8. Lola believed in the _____ of evening schools for working women.

9. The author did not actually _____ the story; she merely related what took place.

10. As a result of her _____, Alma Flor Ada has written many books.

Exercise F ~ Vocabulary Review

Write a complete sentence for each word.

1. exhaustion _____

_____

2. solitary _____

_____

3. responsibility _____

_____

4. malnutrition _____

_____

5. deeds _____

_____

6. vividly _____

_____

7. heroic _____

_____

8. inherited _____

_____

9. recuperate _____

_____

10. topic _____

_____

STUDYING THE STORY

A. Looking Back at the Story

Discuss these questions with your partner or with the group. Your teacher may ask you to write your answer to one or more of the questions.

■ Sometimes we say that a person is "ahead of her (or his) time." What does this mean? How was Grandmother Lola ahead of her time? Find specific examples from the story to support your answer.

■ Suppose that Lola had not called her students' attention to the old man who was walking by. What do you think would have happened to him?

■ Do you agree that life itself was Lola's classroom? Explain.

■ What lesson, or lessons, does "The Teacher" teach?

B. Charting Facts About a Character

In each box in the cluster map below, write a fact about Lola. Some facts might describe the way she looked. Other facts might refer to what she thought and said. Some facts might tell about Lola's actions. You may look back at the story.

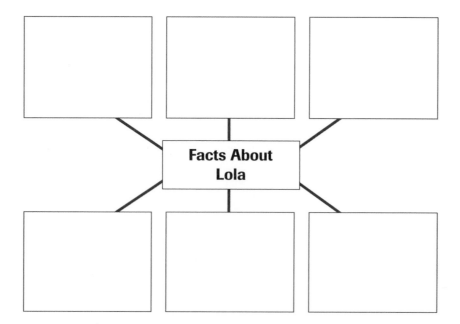

Facts About Lola

THINKING ABOUT LITERATURE

1. Since the **main character** is the person the story is mostly about, Lola is the main character in "The Teacher." Refer to the cluster map on the previous page. Then write a paragraph that tells about Lola. You may use facts that are not on the map.

_____

_____

_____

_____

_____

_____

_____

_____

_____

_____

_____

_____

2. Lola influenced her students and other people she met. Think of a teacher or some other adult who has influenced your life for the better. Tell about that person. Provide facts that **characterize** the individual you chose, and explain how the person affected your life.

_____

_____

_____

_____

_____

_____

_____

_____

_____

_____

_____

_____

_____

_____

3. How well did you grasp the author's **characterization** of the people she wrote about? Fill in the box next to the correct answer.

1. Which expression best characterizes Grandmother Lola?
- ☐ **a.** old, weak, and tired
- ☐ **b.** intelligent, hard-working, and caring
- ☐ **c.** boring and dull

2. When she was teaching a class, Lola
- ☐ **a.** never discussed her thoughts about life.
- ☐ **b.** sometimes used incidents in life as the subject of a lesson.
- ☐ **c.** taught nothing but facts.

3. Lola believed that people should
- ☐ **a.** mind their own business at all times.
- ☐ **b.** think only about themselves.
- ☐ **c.** try to help others.

4. Which did Lola enjoy most?
- ☐ **a.** teaching and telling stories
- ☐ **b.** working on the farm
- ☐ **c.** listening to the radio

As you know, characters sometimes change during a story. The following questions relate to **character development**.

5. When the students first met the old man, he was
- ☐ **a.** cheerful and friendly.
- ☐ **b.** healthy and strong.
- ☐ **c.** very sad and lonely.

6. During the time he spent with the family, the man was
- ☐ **a.** very disappointed.
- ☐ **b.** helpful and happy.
- ☐ **c.** angry and confused.

THE TIGER

BY LIN YUTANG

GETTING READY TO READ

1. The Story and You

In many stories from China, people are magically changed, or
transformed, into animals. This occurs in "The Tiger." Suppose that, for a
brief period of time, you could transform yourself into an animal. What
animal would you choose to be? Explain your decision.

2. Learning About Literature

The **plot** tells the important events that occur in a story. The plot is the
series of incidents in the order in which they take place. As you read
"The Tiger," notice the arrangement of the events in the tale. They make
up the plot.

3. Looking Ahead

Look at the illustration on the left. Does it suggests that the story takes
place in a city or in a rural area? Look at the picture of the tiger at the
bottom of the page. Does it seem wild or tame? Do you think it is likely to
attack? Do you think that the two men in the illustration are friends?
What do you think they are doing, and where do you think they are? Read
on to see if you are right.

THE TIGER

BY LIN YUTANG

There stood the man who had killed his father . . .

Chang Feng was traveling in the southern part of China during the reign of Emperor Yuanho in the year 806. Chang lived in the north and had never been to that part of the country before, so everything was new and fascinating to him.

One day he stopped at an inn in the town of Hengsham. After he unpacked his luggage, he went out to take a walk. The countryside was very green and there was a refreshing breeze that came over the mountain. He strolled on and on, enjoying everything enormously. He felt strangely excited.

It was autumn, and the hillsides glowed with red and gold leaves from the trees. A beautiful white temple stood halfway up the mountain. As the sun began to set, the green and blue and purple colors of the fields mixed with the dazzling red and gold of the trees. It was like a magic land.

Suddenly Chang had a strange sensation. He felt weak. Stars danced before his eyes and he was dizzy. He thought it was due to the altitude, or from the exertion of having walked so much, or perhaps he was affected by the colors and the light.

A few feet in front of him, he saw a pasture that had a thick, soft lawn. He took off his jacket, put it on the grass, and lay down to rest. He felt a little better now. As he looked up at the blue sky, he thought how beautiful and peaceful nature was. Men fought for money and fame. They lied and cheated and killed for gain. But here was peace—in nature. As he lay on the grass, he felt happy and relaxed. The smell of the green grass and a gentle breeze soon put him to sleep.

When he woke up, he felt hungry and realized that it was late in the day. As he rolled his hands over his stomach, he touched soft fur.

Quickly he sat up and saw that his body was covered with beautiful black stripes. As he stretched his arms, he felt a delightful new strength in them, thick and full of power. He yawned and was surprised at his own powerful roar. Looking down at his own face, he saw the tips of long white whiskers. Suddenly he realized that he had been transformed into a tiger!

"Now that is delightful," he thought to himself. "I am no longer a man, but a tiger. It is not bad for a change."

Eager to try his new strength, he ran into the woods and bounced from rock to rock, delighted with his new strength. He went up to the temple and knocked at the door with his paw, seeking to be admitted.

"It is a tiger!" he heard a priest shouting inside. "Do not open the door!"

"Now that is too bad," he thought to himself. "I only wanted to have supper with him and talk for a while. But of course I am a tiger now, and I suppose that makes a difference."

He had an instinct that he should go down the hill to the village and seek food. As he hid behind a hedge on a country path, he saw a young woman passing by.

"I would like to talk to her," he said to himself. But as he started to move toward the woman, she screamed and ran for her life.

"What kind of life is this when everyone thinks you are an enemy?" he wondered. "I would not hurt her."

He continued to walk. But then he realized that he was hungry, very hungry. "I would like a nice fat pig, or a small juicy lamb," he thought to himself. When he thought this, his mouth watered, and he felt ashamed of himself. But there was this terrible hunger gnawing at his stomach, and he knew he had to eat something or die. He searched the village for a pig or calf or even a chicken. But they were all locked up. All doors were shut against him. As he crouched in a dark alley, waiting for some stray animal to wander by, he heard people talking inside their houses. They were talking about a tiger that was loose in the village.

Since there was no food to satisfy his hunger, he went back to the mountain. He lay in wait for something to come his way. All night he waited, but nothing came by. For a while he must have fallen asleep.

He woke up before dawn. Some travelers were beginning to walk along the mountain road. Just then he saw a man run up to the travelers.

"Have you seen Li Wen?" the man breathlessly asked the travelers.

"He was finishing breakfast when we left the inn," said one of the travelers. "He should be coming along in just a few minutes."

"I have been sent to meet him," said the man. "But I have never seen Li Wen before. Is he traveling alone, or is he accompanied by others? Please tell me what he is wearing, so that I will recognize him when he comes along."

"Well," said the traveler, "Li Wen is with two other men. There are three of them traveling together. Li Wen is the one who is dressed in dark green clothing."

As he listened to this conversation, something told the tiger that he must eat Li Wen. Just why he must eat that person he did not know. But he had a very strong feeling that Li Wen was destined to be his first victim. In fact, as the tiger listened to the conversation from his hiding place, it seemed as if it were taking place especially for his benefit. He had never seen or heard of Li Wen in his life and knew nothing about that individual. Still, he crouched in the tall grass and waited for his victim.

Soon he saw Li Wen coming up the road with two other companions. When Li Wen came close enough, the tiger, Chang, rushed out, knocked him to the ground, and carried him up the mountain. The travelers were so frightened that they all ran away. Chang's hunger was satisfied, and he only felt as if he had had a bigger breakfast than usual.

Satisfied with his meal, he lay down to take a nap. When he woke up he thought he must have been crazy to eat a human being who had done him no harm. "I must have been mad to do such a thing," he said to himself. His head cleared and he decided it was not such a pleasant life, prowling night after night for food. He remembered the night before, when hunger drove him to the village and up the mountain, and he could do nothing to stop himself.

"I shall go back to that lawn and see if I can become a human being," he said to himself.

He found the place on the lawn where he had left his jacket. Then he lay down on the lawn, wishing he might wake up and be a man again. He rolled over on the grass and in a few seconds found that he had been changed back to his human shape.

Chang Feng was delighted, but he was puzzled by the strange experience. He put on his jacket and started back to the town. When he reached the inn, he found that he had been gone for exactly twenty-four hours.

"Where have you been?" asked the innkeeper. "We have been searching for you all day. We were extremely worried about you. There was a tiger in the area. He was seen by a woman in the village last night, and this morning, a guest, Li Wen, was eaten by him. I am relieved to see that you have returned here safely."

Chang Feng made up a story that he had spent the night in the temple.

"You are very lucky!" exclaimed the innkeeper, shaking his head. "It was in that vicinity that Li Wen was killed by the tiger."

"No, the tiger will not eat me," Chang Feng replied.

"Why not?"

"He cannot," Chang Feng said mysteriously.

Chang Feng kept the secret to himself, for he certainly could not reveal to anyone what had happened.

Chang Feng went back to his home in Honan, and several years went by. One day he went to Huaiyang, a city on the Huai River. His friends made a dinner party for him and much wine was consumed. Between the courses, the guests were each asked to tell about a strange experience.

Chang Feng began to tell his own story, and it happened that one of the guests was the son of Li Wen, the man he had eaten. As Chang went on with his story, the young man's face grew angrier and angrier.

"So it was you who killed my father!" the young man shouted at him furiously.

Chang Feng quickly stood up and apologized. He knew that he had gotten himself into a very serious situation. "I am sorry," said Chang. "I did not know that it was your father."

The young man suddenly picked up a knife from the table and threw it at Chang. Luckily, it missed and fell with a clang on the floor. The young man rushed at Chang, but the other guests grabbed the man and held him back.

"I will kill you to avenge my father's death! I will follow you to the ends of the earth!" the young man shouted.

The friends persuaded Chang Feng to leave the house at once and told him to hide for a while, while they tried to calm Li Wen's son. Everyone agreed that to avenge one's father's death was a noble thing. But after all, Chang Feng had eaten Li Wen when he was a tiger, and no one wanted to see more blood flow. It was an unusual situation and it raised a difficult question—whether revenge was right in this case under the circumstances. Still, the young man swore to kill Chang to avenge his father's death.

Finally the friends contacted the governor of the region. The governor ordered Li Wen's son to cross the Huai River and never to return. Chang Feng, on his part, changed his name and went to the northern part of the country to keep as far away from his enemy as possible.

When Li Wen's son returned to his home, his friends said to him, "We know how you feel, and we sympathize with you. We understand why you want revenge for your father's death. However, Chang Feng ate your father when he was a tiger and is not responsible for his action. He did not know your father and had no reason to kill him. That was a strange and special case, but he did not plan to murder your father, and if you kill Chang Feng, you will be accused of murder yourself."

The son respected this advice and decided not to hunt down Chang Feng anymore.

Meet the Author

Lin Yutang (1895–1976) gained fame as an author and scholar. Born in Changchow, China, he graduated from college in Shanghai. He later received a degree from Harvard University. After teaching English at the University of Peking, he moved to New York and wrote many novels about Chinese life and culture. One of these, *My Country and My People*, became a best-seller. Some of Lin Yutang's finest stories are collected in *Famous Chinese Short Stories*, from which "The Tiger" is taken.

MAGIC WORDS

BY A NETSILIK ESKIMO

In the very earliest time,
when both people and animals lived on earth,
a person could become an animal if he wanted to
and an animal could become a human being . . .

5   That was the time when words were like magic.
The human mind had mysterious powers.
A word spoken by chance
might have strange consequences.
It would suddenly come alive
10   and what people wanted to happen could happen—
all you had to do was say it.
Nobody could explain this:
That's the way it was.

CHECK YOUR READING

Put an **X** in the box next to the correct answer.

Reading Comprehension

1. "The Tiger" takes place
   - ☐ **a.** in the present.
   - ☐ **b.** about fifty years ago.
   - ☐ **c.** in the year 806.

2. When Chang woke up after his nap, he discovered that he
   - ☐ **a.** was in bed at the inn.
   - ☐ **b.** was no longer in China.
   - ☐ **c.** had become a tiger.

3. When the tiger, Chang, knocked on the door of the temple,
   - ☐ **a.** the priest invited him in.
   - ☐ **b.** the priest refused to open the door.
   - ☐ **c.** the priest ran into the woods.

4. Which statement is true?
   - ☐ **a.** The innkeeper said that he was worried about Chang.
   - ☐ **b.** Chang spent the night in the temple.
   - ☐ **c.** Li Wen was wearing a brown suit.

5. When Chang reached the inn, he discovered that he had been gone for exactly
   - ☐ **a.** an hour.
   - ☐ **b.** eight hours.
   - ☐ **c.** twenty-four hours.

6. The governor told Li Wen's son
   - ☐ **a.** to apologize to Chang.
   - ☐ **b.** to leave and never return.
   - ☐ **c.** to appear in court.

7. At the end of the story, Li Wen's son
   - ☐ **a.** swore he would kill Chang.
   - ☐ **b.** decided not to hunt Chang anymore.
   - ☐ **c.** became one of Chang's best friends.

Vocabulary

8. The tiger crouched in the tall grass and waited for its victim. The word *crouched* means
   - ☐ **a.** bent forward.
   - ☐ **b.** fell asleep.
   - ☐ **c.** ran in circles.

9. Chang didn't like to go prowling night after night for food. The word *prowling* means
   - ☐ **a.** hunting.
   - ☐ **b.** thinking.
   - ☐ **c.** dreaming.

Idioms

10. After his meal, the tiger lay down to take a nap. The idiom *to take a nap* means to
    - ☐ **a.** watch for enemies.
    - ☐ **b.** move from place to place.
    - ☐ **c.** sleep for a short time.

How many questions did you answer correctly? Circle your score. Then fill in your score on the Score Chart on page 184.

Number Correct	Score
1	10
2	20
3	30
4	40
5	50
6	60
7	70
8	80
9	90
10	100

UNDERSTANDING THE STORY

Exercise A ~ Checking Comprehension

Answer each question by writing a complete sentence. Be sure your sentences are grammatically correct. You may look back at the story.

1. When was Chang Feng traveling in the southern part of China?

_____

2. What did Chang do after he unpacked his luggage?

_____

3. What did Chang realize when he woke up after his nap?

_____

4. What happened when the tiger started to move toward the woman?

_____

5. Where did the tiger carry Li Wen?

_____

6. How long had Chang been away from the inn?

_____

7. Where did Chang say he had spent the night?

_____

8. What did Li Wen's son throw at Chang?

_____

9. What did the governor order Li Wen's son to do?

_____

10. What did the young man decide at the end of the story?

_____

Exercise B ~ Adding Vocabulary

In the box are 10 words from the story. Complete each sentence by adding
the correct word.

gnawing	respected	refreshing	avenge	exertion
victim	sympathize	companions	altitude	satisfy

1. Chang felt weak from walking in a place where the

_____ was very high.

2. Perhaps he was dizzy from the _____ of having
walked for so long.

3. A _____ breeze made Chang feel less tired.

4. A terrible hunger was _____ at his stomach, and he
knew he had to eat something or die.

5. He was searching for something to eat so that he could

_____ his hunger.

6. The tiger saw Li Wen walking along the road with two other

_____.

7. The tiger knew that Li Wen would be its first _____.

8. The young man thought that by killing Chang, he would

_____ the death of his father.

9. His friends said to him, "We know how you feel, and we

_____ with you."

10. The young man _____ his friends and followed their
advice.

Exercise C ~ Combining Sentences
Part A

Combine two **simple sentences** into one **compound sentence** by using a comma and the **coordinating conjunction** in parentheses (*and, but, or*). Write the compound sentence on the line. The first one has been done for you.

1. First Chang Feng unpacked his luggage. Then he took a walk in the countryside. (and)

First Chang Feng unpacked his luggage, and then he took a walk in the countryside.

2. The tiger looked for something to eat. It was unable to find anything. (but)

_____

_____

_____

3. Was he tired from walking so far? Was he affected by the color and the light? (or)

_____

_____

_____

4. The tiger started to move toward the woman. She ran away from him. (but)

_____

_____

_____

5. The tiger stayed in the village for a long time. Then it went back to the mountain. (and)

_____

_____

_____

6. Was Li Wen traveling alone? Was he accompanied by others? (or)

_____

_____

_____

7. Chang Feng apologized to the young man. The young man refused to accept the apology. (but)

_____

_____

_____

8. The son went to the southern part of the country. Chang Feng left for the northern part. (and)

_____

_____

_____

9. The young man rushed at Chang. The other guests held him back. (but)

_____

_____

_____

10. You must not kill Chang Feng. You will be accused of murder. (or)

_____

_____

_____

_____

Part B

By combining **simple sentences** into **compound sentences**, you can make your writing stronger and more interesting. Combine the following simple sentences into compound sentences by using a comma and a **coordinating conjunction** (*and*, *but*, *or*). Write the compound sentences on the lines.

1. At first Chang enjoyed being a tiger. Later he regretted it.

_____

_____

_____

2. The villagers were afraid of the tiger. They locked their doors.

_____

_____

_____

3. Did the tiger attack the other travelers? Did it just scare them away?

_____

_____

_____

4. Chang felt sorry for Li Wen. There was nothing he could do now.

_____

_____

_____

5. The son listened to his friends. He didn't bother Chang Feng anymore.

_____

_____

_____

Exercise D ～ Finding Synonyms

Read the sentence. Then select the **synonym** (the word most similar in meaning) for the word in capital letters. Put an **X** in the box next to the correct answer. Each capitalized word appears in the story.

1. Chang Feng was traveling in the southern part of China during the reign of Emperor Yuanho.

   REIGN
   - ☐ **a.** rule
   - ☐ **b.** city
   - ☐ **c.** leader

2. After Chang arrived at the inn, he unpacked his luggage and went outside.

   LUGGAGE
   - ☐ **a.** food
   - ☐ **b.** pockets
   - ☐ **c.** baggage

3. Chang strolled on and on, enjoying everything that he saw.

   STROLLED
   - ☐ **a.** talked
   - ☐ **b.** walked
   - ☐ **c.** dreamed

4. Chang suddenly realized that he had been transformed into a tiger.

   TRANSFORMED
   - ☐ **a.** attacked
   - ☐ **b.** worried
   - ☐ **c.** changed

5. He was puzzled by the strange experience.

   PUZZLED
   - ☐ **a.** confused
   - ☐ **b.** helped
   - ☐ **c.** learned

6. The tiger had a strong feeling that it was destined to kill Li Wen.

   DESTINED
   - ☐ **a.** warned
   - ☐ **b.** permitted
   - ☐ **c.** fated

7. Everyone agreed that correcting a wrong was a noble thing to do.

   NOBLE
   - ☐ **a.** honorable
   - ☐ **b.** small
   - ☐ **c.** interesting

8. Chang was invited to a dinner party where much wine was consumed.

   CONSUMED
   - ☐ **a.** dropped
   - ☐ **b.** drunk
   - ☐ **c.** sent

9. Chang's friends persuaded him to leave the house at once.

   PERSUADED
   - ☐ **a.** watched
   - ☐ **b.** convinced
   - ☐ **c.** guessed

10. Because of the unusual circumstances, the son was not allowed to track down the man who had killed his father.

   CIRCUMSTANCES
   - ☐ **a.** conditions
   - ☐ **b.** threats
   - ☐ **c.** times

Exercise E ~ Finding Antonyms

Antonyms are words with opposite meanings. For example, the words *rich* and *poor* and *slow* and *fast* are antonyms. Read the sentence. Then select the antonym for the word in capital letters. Put an **X** in the box next to the correct answer. Each capitalized word appears in the story.

1. Chang Feng lay down to rest and felt happy and relaxed.

RELAXED
- [ ] **a.** calm
- [ ] **b.** tired
- [ ] **c.** nervous

2. When he became a tiger, Chang was surprised at the strength in his arms.

STRENGTH
- [ ] **a.** length
- [ ] **b.** weakness
- [ ] **c.** power

*Did you select the **antonym**—the word that was opposite in meaning?*

3. Since Chang did not want to kill anyone, he was ashamed of his actions.

ASHAMED
- [ ] **a.** proud
- [ ] **b.** embarrassed
- [ ] **c.** exhausted

4. He was eager to discover the new powers he possessed.

EAGER
- [ ] **a.** determined
- [ ] **b.** excited
- [ ] **c.** reluctant

5. The tiger crouched in the tall grass and then pounced on its victim.

VICTIM
- [ ] **a.** prey
- [ ] **b.** attacker
- [ ] **c.** enemy

6. He kept the secret to himself and did not reveal what had happened.

REVEAL
- [ ] **a.** conceal
- [ ] **b.** excuse
- [ ] **c.** tell

7. Everyone agreed that to avenge a father's death was a noble thing to do.

NOBLE
- [ ] **a.** surprising
- [ ] **b.** gallant
- [ ] **c.** rude

8. Chang was amazed when he discovered that he had been transformed into a tiger.

TRANSFORMED
- [ ] **a.** altered
- [ ] **b.** unchanged
- [ ] **c.** assisted

Exercise F ~ Vocabulary Review

Write a complete sentence for each word or idiom.

1. crouched _____

_____

2. prowling _____

_____

3. sympathize _____

_____

4. companions _____

_____

5. reign _____

_____

6. destined _____

_____

7. circumstances _____

_____

8. victim _____

_____

9. exertion _____

_____

10. took a nap (idiom) _____

_____

STUDYING THE STORY

A. Looking Back at the Story

Discuss these questions with your partner or with the group. Your teacher may ask you to write your answer to one or more of the questions.

■ "The Tiger" is a strange and unusual story. In what ways is it different from most stories you have read?

■ The young man was told by his friends, "Chang Feng ate your father when he was a tiger and is not responsible for his actions." Do you agree, or do you believe that Chang should have been responsible for the death of Li Wen? Why? Explain.

■ Do you think the young man should have listened to his friends, or should he have attempted to hunt down Chang Feng? Give reasons for your answers.

B. Charting the Story

As you know, the **plot** tells the important incidents and events that take place, or occur, in the story. Look back at "The Tiger" to obtain the information you need to complete the plot in the story map below.

The Tiger

Main Character:
Chang Feng

Plot (important events that take place in the story):

1. _____

2. _____

3. _____

4. _____

5. _____

6. _____

7. _____

8. _____

THINKING ABOUT LITERATURE

1. A **summary** tells the main, or the most important, events in a story. Use the events in the plot on the chart you completed to help you write a summary of "The Tiger." You may include other events that do not appear on the chart.

_____

_____

_____

_____

_____

_____

_____

_____

2. Now it's time for you to be a character in the story. Suppose you were a guest at the dinner party where Chang Feng told his story. On the lines below, describe what happened. Make your **description** as complete and as vivid as possible.

_____

_____

_____

_____

_____

_____

(Continue your story on the following page).

_____

_____

_____

_____

_____

_____

_____

3. As you know, the **plot** is the series of incidents or events in a story. See how well you understood the plot of "The Tiger." Fill in the box next to the correct answer.

1. What happened first in the plot of the story?
- ☐ **a.** The tiger waited in the tall grass for Li Wen.
- ☐ **b.** Li Wen's son threw a knife at Chang Feng.
- ☐ **c.** Chang Feng was tired and fell asleep on the grass.

2. What happened last in the plot of the story?
- ☐ **a.** Li Wen's son returned home and spoke to his friends.
- ☐ **b.** The tiger knocked on the door of the temple.
- ☐ **c.** The innkeeper said that they had searched for Chang all day.

3. Which one of the following events plays the most important part in the plot of the story?
- ☐ **a.** The priest heard a tiger knocking at the door.
- ☐ **b.** The tiger, Chang, ate Li Wen.
- ☐ **c.** Chang Feng decided to change his name.

4. As a result of which event did Li Wen's son learn that Chang was responsible for the death of his father?
- ☐ **a.** Chang told the story at a dinner party that the son attended.
- ☐ **b.** Some travelers told the son what had happened.
- ☐ **c.** The innkeeper gave this information to the son.

4. Magic Words

a. Read the poem again. How could people become animals and animals become people?

_____

_____

_____

_____

b. Suppose that a time actually existed when people could become animals and animals could become people. Do you think you would have liked living then? Why?

_____

_____

_____

_____

c. The poet says that words once had magic powers. Do words have "magic power" today? Think about TV, movies, stories, and books. Explain your answer.

_____

_____

_____

_____

d. Why do you think "Magic Words" appears in a unit with "The Tiger"?

_____

_____

_____

_____

AFTER TWENTY YEARS

BY O. HENRY

GETTING READY TO READ

1. The Story and You

In this story, two friends agree to go their own ways and to meet again "after twenty years." At that time, they will learn how their lives have changed. What do you think *your* life will be like five years from now? Ten years? Twenty years from now? You might want to discuss such things as the job you will have and where you think you will be living.

2. Learning About Literature

O. Henry is famous for writing stories that conclude with a **surprise ending**. In fact, the surprise ending has become O. Henry's "trademark." It is featured in all of his short stories. A surprise ending means that the ending is different from what most readers expect, or anticipate. However, the author usually provides clues and hints to help the reader guess and understand the surprise. As you read "After Twenty Years," look for the clues that will help you infer (figure out by reasoning) the ending to the story.

3. Looking Ahead

Look at the illustration on the left. Do you think the story takes place during the day or at night—in the country or in a city? Why might the time of day be important? When do you think the action in the story occurs—now, in the future, or at some time in the past? How do you know? Look at the face of the man in the picture. Judging by the man's expression, how does he feel? What might the man be thinking about? (Remember that the story is called "After Twenty Years.") Do you think the man is rich or poor? How old do you think he is? Read on to see if you are right.

AFTER TWENTY YEARS

BY O. HENRY

Twenty years can change a man . . .

The time was nearly ten o'clock at night, and the streets were almost deserted. Strong gusts of wind and the threat of rain had forced most people to stay indoors. The police officer on the beat[1] moved slowly up the avenue. The guardian of the peace tried doors as he went and looked in store windows along the way.

Most of the places in the vicinity were closed. Now and then you might see lights in a luncheonette that stayed open all night, but the majority of the doors belonged to businesses that had been shut for hours.

In the middle of a certain block, the officer suddenly slowed his walk. In the dark doorway of a hardware store a man stood, with an unlighted cigar in his mouth. As the police officer walked up to him, the man spoke up quickly.

"It's all right, officer," the man said reassuringly. "I'm just waiting for a friend. It's an appointment that we made twenty years ago."

The officer looked surprised and stared at the man.

"I guess it sounds a little funny to you, doesn't it?" said the man. "Well, I can explain it. Twenty years ago there used to be a restaurant where this store is now."

"Yes," said the officer. "That was Joe Brady's Restaurant. It was here until five years ago. It was torn down then."

The man in the doorway struck a match and lit his cigar. The officer saw that the man had a pale, square face with keen eyes. There was a little scar near the man's right eyebrow. The man was wearing a scarf whose ends were held together by a shiny gold pin.

---

1. *beat*: As used here, the word means "a usual route or way of going."

In the center of the pin was a large, sparkling diamond.

The man said, "Exactly twenty years ago tonight I ate dinner with Jimmy Wells at Joe Brady's Restaurant here. Jimmy was my best friend and the greatest pal in the world. He and I were born in New York and grew up together. We were as close as two brothers."

The man in the doorway paused for a moment as he thought about his friend. Then he continued.

"I was eighteen and Jimmy was twenty. The next morning I was going to leave for the West to make my fortune. But you couldn't have dragged Jimmy out of New York. He thought it was the best place on earth. Well, we agreed that night that we would meet here again *exactly twenty years* from that date and time, no matter how our lives had changed, or how far we had to travel. We figured that in twenty years each of us would have his destiny worked out, whatever it might be."

"That sounds pretty interesting to me," said the officer. "But twenty years is a long time to wait before getting together. Have you heard from your friend?"

"Well, yes, for a while we corresponded. But after a year or two we stopped writing and didn't keep in touch with each other. You see, the West is a pretty big place, and I kept moving around all the time. But I know that Jimmy will meet me here if he's alive. He was always the truest, most reliable guy in the world. He'll never forget! I came a thousand miles to stand in this doorway tonight—and it will be worth it if my old friend shows up."

The man pulled out a handsome gold watch. The officer saw that the hands of the watch were made of small diamonds.

"It's three minutes before ten," the man in the doorway announced. "It was exactly ten o'clock when we left the restaurant twenty years ago."

"You did pretty well out West, didn't you?" asked the officer.

"Oh, yes! I certainly did! I hope Jimmy has done half as well. He was never as bold as me, though. I've had to compete with some of the smartest guys around. But I took some chances, made a lot of money, and came out on top. You have to be pretty sharp to do well in New York, but out West I learned how to be as sharp as a razor."

The police officer took a step or two.

"Well," he said, "I'll be going now. I hope that your friend shows up. Are you going to leave if he doesn't get here on time?"

"No, not at all," the other man said. "I'll wait at least another half an hour. If Jimmy is alive on earth, he'll be here by then. Good night, officer."

"Good night, sir," said the officer, and he moved on, trying doors as he went.

There was now a light, cold drizzle falling and the wind was beginning to blow harder. The few people in the street hurried silently and dismally along, their coat collars pulled up, their hands in their pockets. And in the doorway of the hardware store stood the man who had come a thousand miles to keep an appointment he had made twenty years go. He smoked his cigar and he waited.

He waited about twenty minutes. Then a tall man in a long overcoat, with the collar turned up to his ears, hurried across from the opposite side of the street. The tall man went straight to the man who was waiting in the doorway.

The tall man paused and then asked, "Is that you—Bob?"

"Jimmy Wells! Is that you?" exclaimed the man in the doorway. "I was sure you would come!"

The man who had just arrived threw his arms around the other man, and shook his hand. "Bob!" he said. "I was certain I would find you here if you were still alive. Well, well, well!—twenty years is a long time. The old restaurant is gone, Bob. I wish it were still here, so we could enjoy another dinner there now."

The tall man stepped back and asked, "How has the West treated you, old pal?"

"Great! It has given me everything I wanted. You've changed quite a bit, Jimmy. You look two or three inches taller than I remembered."

"Oh, I grew a few inches after I was twenty."

"Are you doing well in New York, Jimmy?"

"Fairly well," said the tall man. "I have a job in one of the city's departments. Come on, Bob. We'll go to a place I know, and have a good long talk about old times."

The two men walked up the street, arm in arm. The man from the West, extremely pleased with his success, was talking about himself in a rather conceited way. The other man, submerged in his overcoat, listened with interest.

At the corner stood a drugstore that was bright with lights. When they came into this glare, each man turned simultaneously to look at the other man's face.

The man from the West stopped suddenly and released the other man's arm.

"You're not Jimmy Wells!" he exclaimed in distress. "Twenty years is a long time. But it's not long enough to change the shape of a man's nose."

"It sometimes changes a good man into a bad one," said the tall man.

The tall man put his arm on the other man's shoulder and said, "You've been under arrest for ten minutes, 'Silky' Bob. We heard from the Chicago police that you were heading our way, and they want to have a little talk with you there. Going quietly, are you? That's sensible. Now before we go to the station, here's a note I was asked to give to you. It's from Officer Wells."

The man from the West looked at the piece of paper the tall man gave him. His hand was steady when he began to read, but it trembled a little by the time he had finished. The note was very short.

> Bob: I was at the meeting place on time. When you struck the match to light your cigar, I saw that you were the man wanted for robbery in Chicago. Somehow, I couldn't arrest you myself. So I went and got a detective to do the job.
>
> Jimmy

You can **infer**, or figure out, that Officer Jimmy Wells did at least two things after he recognized "Silky" Bob. One thing Wells did was to send a detective to make the arrest. What else did Wells do? When you **make an inference**, you use clues or information in the story to reach a decision.

Meet the Author

O. Henry (1862–1910) is the pen name of William Sidney Porter, one of America's most popular short-story writers. Born in Greensboro, North Carolina, O. Henry eventually moved to New York City, the setting of many of his 300 stories. He wrote his first stories in an Ohio prison, where he served three years for stealing money while working as a bank teller. It is not clear if O. Henry actually stole the funds, but he fled the country and was arrested and sentenced when he returned. He subsequently took his pen name from a prison guard named Orrin Henry. O. Henry's stories are famous for the author's trademark—the surprise ending.

CHECK YOUR READING

Put an **X** in the box next to the correct answer.

Reading Comprehension

1. The police officer saw a man standing in the doorway of
☐ **a.** a restaurant.
☐ **b.** a hardware store.
☐ **c.** a drugstore.

2. How far had the man come to meet his old friend?
☐ **a.** a hundred miles
☐ **b.** five hundred miles
☐ **c.** a thousand miles

3. How long ago had the man made the appointment?
☐ **a.** ten years ago
☐ **b.** twenty years ago
☐ **c.** twenty-five years ago

4. How much longer was the man willing to wait for his friend?
☐ **a.** a few minutes
☐ **b.** at least half an hour
☐ **c.** all night

5. Where was Jimmy born?
☐ **a.** in New Jersey
☐ **b.** in New York
☐ **c.** somewhere in the West

6. Bob thought that his friend looked
☐ **a.** taller.
☐ **b.** shorter.
☐ **c.** thinner.

Vocabulary

7. At the corner, the glare from a drugstore shone through the darkness. As used here, the word *glare* means
☐ **a.** windows.
☐ **b.** items for sale.
☐ **c.** a bright light.

8. Each man turned simultaneously to look at the other man's face. The word *simultaneously* means
☐ **a.** at the same time.
☐ **b.** very slowly.
☐ **c.** without interest.

Idioms

9. After a while, they stopped writing and didn't keep in touch with each other. The idiom *to keep in touch with* means to
☐ **a.** communicate with.
☐ **b.** think about.
☐ **c.** need help.

10. The officer said, "I hope that your friend shows up." As used here, the idiom *shows up* means
☐ **a.** remembers.
☐ **b.** appears.
☐ **c.** waits.

How many questions did you answer correctly? Circle your score. Then fill in your score on the Score Chart on page 184.

Number Correct	Score
1	10
2	20
3	30
4	40
5	50
6	60
7	70
8	80
9	90
10	100

UNDERSTANDING THE STORY

Exercise A ~ Checking Comprehension

Answer each question by writing a complete sentence. Be sure your sentences are grammatically correct. You may look back at the story.

1. What did the police officer do as he walked along?

2. What did the man in the doorway have in his mouth?

3. How long ago had the man made the appointment?

4. When was Joe Brady's Restaurant torn down?

5. How old was the man when he left for the West?

6. Why didn't Jimmy want to leave New York?

7. How much longer was the man willing to wait for his friend?

8. Where did the tall man work?

9. How long had "Silky" Bob been under arrest?

10. What did Jimmy realize when Bob lit his cigar?

Exercise B ~ Adding Vocabulary

In the box are 10 words from the story. Complete each sentence by adding the correct word.

scar	compete	reassuringly	conceited	razor
destiny	gusts	distress	deserted	sparkling

1. Since it was a cold, rainy evening, the streets were almost

_____ .

2. The threat of rain and strong _____ of wind kept most people indoors.

3. "It's all right, officer," the man said _____ .

4. There was a little _____ near the man's right eyebrow.

5. They believed that after twenty years each man would have his

_____ worked out.

6. In the center of the gold pin was a large _____ diamond.

7. He did well, though he had to _____ with some very smart people.

8. In the West, Bob learned how to be "as sharp as a

_____ ."

9. He was extremely pleased with his success and was very

_____ .

10. "You're not Jimmy Wells!" he exclaimed in _____ .

Exercise C ~ Finding Synonyms

Read the sentence. Then select the **synonym** (the word most similar in meaning) for the word in capital letters. Put an **X** in the box next to the correct answer. Each capitalized word appears in the story.

1. Since it was ten o'clock at night, most of the places in the vicinity were closed.

VICINITY
- ☐ **a.** homes
- ☐ **b.** city
- ☐ **c.** neighborhood

2. O. Henry calls a police officer "the guardian of the peace."

GUARDIAN
- ☐ **a.** protector
- ☐ **b.** fighter
- ☐ **c.** hunter

3. The majority of the doors belonged to businesses that had been shut for hours.

MAJORITY
- ☐ **a.** most
- ☐ **b.** some
- ☐ **c.** none

4. He had come to keep an appointment they had made twenty years ago.

APPOINTMENT
- ☐ **a.** discussion
- ☐ **b.** meeting
- ☐ **c.** problem

5. The man from the West had a pale, square face with keen eyes.

KEEN
- ☐ **a.** sleepy
- ☐ **b.** closed
- ☐ **c.** sharp

6. Bob thought that Jimmy was the truest, most reliable friend in the world.

RELIABLE
- ☐ **a.** wealthy
- ☐ **b.** dependable
- ☐ **c.** intelligent

7. A cold drizzle was falling, and the wind began to blow harder.

DRIZZLE
- ☐ **a.** snow
- ☐ **b.** rain
- ☐ **c.** leaves

8. After Bob left for the West, he and Jimmy corresponded for a while.

CORRESPONDED
- ☐ **a.** wrote
- ☐ **b.** argued
- ☐ **c.** searched

9. He didn't think that his friend was as bold as he was.

BOLD
- ☐ **a.** fearless
- ☐ **b.** calm
- ☐ **c.** afraid

10. The man was submerged in a long overcoat with the collar turned up.

SUBMERGED
- ☐ **a.** warm
- ☐ **b.** hidden
- ☐ **c.** obvious

Exercise D ~ Finding Antonyms

As you know, **antonyms** are words with opposite meanings. For example, the words *weak* and *strong* and *up* and *down* are antonyms. Read the sentence. Then select the antonym for the word in capital letters. Put an **X** in the box next to the correct answer. Each capitalized word appears in the story.

1. The police officer thought that the man's story was interesting.

   INTERESTING
   - ☐ **a.** boring
   - ☐ **b.** amusing
   - ☐ **c.** fascinating

2. The man was wearing a handsome gold watch with diamonds.

   HANDSOME
   - ☐ **a.** beautiful
   - ☐ **b.** expensive
   - ☐ **c.** ugly

*Did you select the **antonym**—the word that was opposite in meaning?*

3. The man from the West was pleased with his success and was talking about himself.

   SUCCESS
   - ☐ **a.** wealth
   - ☐ **b.** luck
   - ☐ **c.** failure

4. In the street people hurried silently and dismally through the rain.

   DISMALLY
   - ☐ **a.** cheerfully
   - ☐ **b.** sadly
   - ☐ **c.** slowly

5. Bob suddenly released the other man's arm.

   RELEASED
   - ☐ **a.** dropped
   - ☐ **b.** held
   - ☐ **c.** hit

6. A man hurried across from the opposite side of the street.

   OPPOSITE
   - ☐ **a.** same
   - ☐ **b.** different
   - ☐ **c.** wide

7. His hand was steady when he began reading the letter, but it trembled a little by the time he finished.

   STEADY
   - ☐ **a.** firm
   - ☐ **b.** shaking
   - ☐ **c.** pointing

8. It was sensible for the man to go quietly with the detective.

   SENSIBLE
   - ☐ **a.** smart
   - ☐ **b.** foolish
   - ☐ **c.** unusual

Exercise E ~ Thinking Critically

How well can you "read between the lines"? The following questions will give you opportunities to make inferences, draw conclusions, and use hints and clues found in the story. Fill in the box next to the correct answer.

1. We may conclude that the police officer at the beginning of the story was
- ☐ **a.** Jimmy Wells.
- ☐ **b.** a detective.
- ☐ **c.** Joe Brady.

2. We may infer that Jimmy Wells
- ☐ **a.** hated "Silky" Bob.
- ☐ **b.** was planning to change his job.
- ☐ **c.** felt sad about having his old friend arrested.

3. Which of the following is a clue that the man in the overcoat was not Jimmy Wells?
- ☐ **a.** The man was much heavier than Jimmy.
- ☐ **b.** The man was shorter than Jimmy.
- ☐ **c.** The man was taller than Jimmy.

4. Which of the following is a clue that the man in the overcoat worked for the police?
- ☐ **a.** The man said that he had a job in a city department.
- ☐ **b.** The man looked like a detective.
- ☐ **c.** The man was very tall.

5. We may infer that the officer asked "Silky" Bob how long he would wait for his friend because Jimmy
- ☐ **a.** wanted to make sure that Bob would be there when the detective arrived.
- ☐ **b.** was planning to come back in a few minutes.
- ☐ **c.** was afraid that Bob was getting cold.

6. When Bob was out West, he "kept moving around all the time." We may infer that Bob
- ☐ **a.** could never find a place that he liked.
- ☐ **b.** couldn't afford to pay his rent.
- ☐ **c.** kept moving to stay ahead of the police.

7. The name "Silky" Bob suggests that Bob was
- ☐ **a.** not very smart.
- ☐ **b.** very smooth and clever.
- ☐ **c.** rough and tough.

Exercise F ~ Vocabulary Review

Write a complete sentence for each word or idiom.

1. simultaneously _____

_____

2. conceited _____

_____

3. gusts _____

_____

4. deserted _____

_____

5. compete _____

_____

6. distress _____

_____

7. corresponded _____

_____

8. submerged _____

_____

9. dismally _____

_____

10. kept in touch with (idiom) _____

_____

STUDYING THE STORY

A. Looking Back at the Story

Discuss these questions with your partner or with the group. Your teacher may ask you to write your answer to one or more of the questions.

- What is the **surprise ending** to "After Twenty Years"? The story takes place on a very dark night. Explain in detail why this is very important.

- How did Jimmy feel about having his old friend arrested? Refer to specific items in the story to support your answer.

- "Silky" Bob believed that he was extremely successful. Do you think that he was? Explain your answer.

- Was Jimmy Wells right to place justice over friendship? Why? If you were Jimmy, how would you have handled the situation?

B. Comparing and Contrasting Characters

A **Venn diagram** shows how two characters in a story are different and alike. Look at the Venn diagram below. There are two circles that overlap each other in the middle. In the space in the middle, list all the things that Jimmy Wells and "Silky" Bob have in common—how they are *alike*. Then, in the spaces under their names, list how they are *different*. When you show how characters are alike and different, you **compare** and **contrast** them.

Different	Alike	Different
Jimmy Wells		"Silky" Bob

THINKING ABOUT LITERATURE

1. On the lines below, **compare and contrast** Jimmy Wells and "Silky"
Bob. Refer to the Venn diagram to assist you.

_____

_____

_____

_____

_____

_____

_____

_____

_____

_____

_____

_____

_____

_____

2. Now it's time for you to write your own ending to the story. Bob said that he was willing to wait for his friend "at least another half an hour." Suppose Bob had told the officer that he was going to leave in two minutes. How do you think the story would have ended? Use your imagination. Then try to write your own **surprise ending** to the story. Be sure to put the **dialogue** (the words that the characters say) in quotation marks.

_____

_____

_____

_____

_____

_____

_____

_____

_____

_____

_____

_____

_____

3. At the conclusion of "After Twenty Years," "Silky" Bob reads a note that was sent to him by Officer Wells. Suppose that two years have passed and that Bob writes a note to Jimmy Wells. What do you think Bob might say? Try not to have Bob express anger in his note.

Dear Jimmy,

_____

_____

_____

_____

_____

_____

_____

_____

_____

_____

_____

_____

_____

_____

Bob

THE
STOVE

BASED ON A STORY BY
MARJORIE PICKTHALL

GETTING READY
TO READ

1. The Story and You

In this story, Dorette must take care of her brother who is very ill. To save his life, it is necessary for her to overcome serious obstacles. Identify a situation in which you, or someone you know, faced a difficult problem or had to overcome an obstacle. Explain whether you or the other person handled the challenge successfully. Give details in your answer.

2. Learning About Literature

In literature, **conflict** occurs when there is a struggle, a fight, or a strong difference of opinion between characters. Conflict also occurs when a character clashes, or struggles, with a force of nature. As you might expect, conflict in a story generally leads to action. When you read "The Stove," look for conflict between characters. See if a conflict with nature also plays an important part in the story.

3. Looking Ahead

Look at the illustration on the left. In what kind of building do you think the story takes place? Do you think the building is in a city or in the wilderness? What is probably true about the weather outside? How do you know? Notice that the stove is pictured in two places in the illustration. What do you think the stove uses for fuel? What might happen if the stove went out? In one section of the illustration are the stove, an ax, and furniture, in pieces. What do those objects suggest? Read on to see if you are right.

THE STOVE

BASED ON A STORY BY
MARJORIE PICKTHALL

Nothing could satisfy the great iron stove . . .

I 'll be back with the doctor in three days at the latest. I've left you enough wood for three days and you have plenty of food." Garth looked at his sister anxiously. Suddenly he leaned forward and brushed her cheek lightly with his thick, yellow beard. "I hate to leave you," he said gently, "but I guess it's Derek's only chance."

"Of course you must go. It's Derek's only chance." Dorette faced her brother. Pale and thin, she looked weak, but she was born in the wilderness and possessed a spirit of steel.

She said quietly, "There'll be nothing for me to do, nothing— but wait."

"Only look after yourself and keep the stove going."

"I'll do it. And you—if you meet Martin Dufour—"

Rage suddenly blazed in her brother's eyes. The barrel of his rifle gleamed as he gripped it. "If I meet Martin Dufour," he said through his teeth, "it will be the end of him—or me!"

He turned without saying another word and headed down the forest trail on his way to Mandore.

Dorette watched him until he was just a dark shadow among the trees. All sound, all movement seemed to go with him. She knew that all around her, mile after mile, there was nothing but silence— the silence of the lonely and desolate forest of the North. She went into the cabin and locked the door behind her, as if the loneliness were an enemy she had to keep out.

The cabin was a pleasant place. The walls were made of red cedar, and there were four rugs on the floor and red curtains on the windows. The cabin was divided into two rooms. In the center of the larger room stood the great iron stove. In the winter that stove kept them alive.

The roar of the stove filled the cabin like a hungry voice. Dorette swung open the heavy door and felt the heat on her face as she flung

in some wood to feed the fire. That was her job now until Garth
came back—feeding the stove.

She went to one of the bunks and looked down. Derek, her
younger brother, lay in the bed without moving. He had been that
way ever since Garth and the men had carried him in and put him
there. He had been shot, and drowsed between life and death. From
time to time he sipped a little soup, unaware that someone was
feeding him. Dorette did not dare to touch him. There was nothing
she could do for him but make sure that the cabin was warm enough
to keep him alive until the doctor came, for the cold of that country
kills like a sword.

At the side of the bunk she whispered, "If only you could speak to
me, Derek. If only I could hear your voice."

But the only voice was the voice of the great iron stove.

She thought about the scene Garth had described to her. How
Garth and the men had tracked the outlaw, Martin Dufour, to a
lonely little shack in the snow. How Garth had shouted for Martin to
come out of the shack. How a shot had come from nowhere, striking
Derek. How the men had rushed into the shack and found it empty.
Martin Dufour had escaped again! She saw it all. In her mind she saw
the scene she had not witnessed. And she heard Garth's hard voice
again. "But he's not going to get away this time. He'll have to get
food and shelter somewhere. And if it's a thousand miles away, we'll
follow and shoot him down like the wolf he is!"

She glanced around, shaken, thinking that she still heard Garth's
voice filled with bitter rage. But it was only the roaring stove

humming its angry song.

She busied herself, doing whatever work she could find. Twice she fed the stove from the pile of wood on the floor beside it. The fierce heat licked out at her each time, like a savage beast striking through the bars of its cage. Each time she shut the door, she felt as though she were locking up some living thing.

She glanced at the clock. Only an hour of the slow time had passed. Garth had been gone only an hour. She turned the clock toward the wall, took out a shirt she was making for Garth, and started to stitch it.

As she worked, she heard the soft thud of snow falling from trees in the forest. She could hear Derek's weak, shallow breathing. Now and then his heart seemed to pause. Then she held her breath until her brother's heart resumed its weak rhythm.

So the morning passed. In the afternoon she found a snowshoe that needed restringing. She twisted the gut and wove the net, working carefully on it.

It was dark sooner than she could have hoped. The stove filled the cabin with its glow. Glancing at the windows, she saw that they were covered with frost. It would be a cold night. She thought about Garth and then—with dread—about Martin Dufour. She dragged her cot from the other room, set it in front of the stove, and lay down. The warmth was like a hand pressing on her eyelids.

Five times during the long night, she woke up to feed the stove. The last time she awoke, the sun had risen. The frost on the window was glowing. Dorette went into the other room and combed her hair.

That day passed as the first had done, although it seemed to her that her brother looked weaker. She pleaded with him, "Take a mouthful of soup. Take it for my sake, Derek." But her voice could not reach him.

The diminished heap of logs on the floor showed that there was work for her to do. She must bring in a fresh supply from the pile of firewood behind the cabin. She ate a quick breakfast. Then, putting on her coat and hood to protect herself from the cold, she opened the door.

She stepped into a world of white, blue, and black; a world sparkling brilliantly as though made of gems. It was fiercely cold. She shut the door behind her, ran quickly to the snow-buried woodpile behind the cabin, and gathered an armful of small logs. Then she returned to the cabin, pushed open the door, and tumbled the wood onto the floor. She worked that way all morning. As she did her

spirits rose, and she began to feel better. She began to believe that
Derek would not die, and remembered that Garth would return soon.
She was pleased with the crashing noise the logs made as she threw
them on the floor. It was a change from the one unceasing voice that
filled the cabin day and night—the voice of the stove.

The second night she was restless. At first she dared not sleep, for
fear that she would sleep too soundly. She could hear the wind
whistling loudly. The great stove sang to a higher note. She could
hardly keep up with its consuming hunger. The pine and birch logs
burned to ashes in minutes. When she did sleep, she dreamed that
the cold was creeping into the cabin in long fingers of frost that
twisted, like snakes, under the door. One touched her on the throat
and she woke up, choking.

Dawn found the sky filled with clouds, the cabin warm, the sick
man still alive.

As the day went on her heart grew lighter. In four or five hours
Garth should be back with the doctor from Mandore. She wound the
clock and turned it so that it faced the room. She no longer dreaded
seeing the passage of time.

Five hours went by and Garth had not yet arrived.

She went to the door. Closing it behind her to prevent the cold
from entering the cabin for even a moment, she stared down the trail.
It ran straight for less than half a mile; beyond that she could not see.

"Garth! Garth! Garth!"

Who had uttered that wild cry that echoed among the trees? She paused for a moment. Then she realized that it had come from her!

She decided she must see beyond the bend in the trail. She built up the fire, put on her coat and hood and snowshoes, took a glance at Derek, and left the cabin. She sped down the trail. She was panting when she reached the curve. Almost afraid to look, she saw the long track of footprints in the snow leading away. She saw nothing else. She did not dare to go on. She turned around and ran home.

The clock ticked off another hour—two, three, four. Garth had not returned.

Darkness, and he had not come.

Loneliness and suspense were shaking her strong, young nerves. Worst of all was the silence. The voice of the stove was at first annoying; then it became intolerable. She threw the wood in angrily. "If there was only someone to *speak* to," she said a little wildly—"just someone to give me a word!"

There was no one then—nor through the endless night.

She stayed awake all night, afraid to fall asleep, fearful that the stove that kept them alive might go out. Dawn came and Garth still was not there.

There was no wood left in the cabin. Before she did anything else, she put on her coat and went back to the woodpile.

The wood was piled high against the back of the cabin and was covered with snow. She pulled at a log and the wood came tumbling down. The hard work was a relief to her as she piled a load so heavy, she swayed under its weight. "It's something I can do for Derek," she said. "It's all I can do."

She took in enough for the day. But there was the night.

"Garth will be back by then," she muttered, staring at the stove. Just then the stove sent a screaming rush of flame up the pipe, as though it were mocking her. She felt a hatred for it as she went wearily out again to gather enough wood for the night too.

She kneeled beside the woodpile and reached in for the logs. She felt nothing but snow!

She pushed her arm into the snow up to her shoulder. Still she felt nothing but snow.

Her heart began to pound loudly. She found a long stick and prodded the pile, but still she found nothing but snow.

"How did it happen?" she asked herself over and over. Easily enough. She or Garth or Derek had been taking logs from the other side of the pile. A large drift of snow had slipped down from the roof and had filled the empty spaces in the pile. What they believed were logs was no more than a huge heap of snow.

Dorette turned slowly and went into the cabin.

She stood near Derek's bunk and stared at the wood on the floor. It was enough for the day, but what about the night?

Would Garth return before the night?

She looked around the cabin. There were things there, things that would burn. Her brown eyes grew wider. There was war in them as she leaned over and kissed Derek's cheek. He did not stir from his sleep.

"Sleep well, Derek," she whispered. "I'll take care of you."

She took Garth's heavy ax and began on the chairs.

They were heavy and clumsy things. Garth had made them himself and was proud of them. Still, they would feed the stove well. But they were hard and difficult to chop, and Dorette's hands had been scorched by the door of the stove. As she toiled, striking each blow sharply and cleanly, her eyes searched the cabin for firewood. That box could be used, that shelf, the table. The wind howled loudly outside and the day was full of sounds. Now and then she ran to the door, crying, "Garth!" But each time she saw nothing but the forest and the snow.

By early evening she had chopped up everything in the cabin. Each stroke sent pain to her shoulder from her burned and bruised hands, but she did not feel it. And still the stove roared, ever hungry. The dry wood from the cabin burned quickly, like straw. The great iron stove must be fed, and she had nothing to feed it!

She took the ax and went out.

The gray forest stood before her in snow and in shadows. There must be a hundred fallen boughs[1] within range of the cabin. She

----

1. *boughs*: very large branches of a tree

found one and dragged it from the snow into the cabin. She tore off the branches and thrust them into the stove. Blood from her hands stained the wood that she threw into the fire.

She went out again. There was a large branch hanging down from a spruce. She tore at it desperately with all her strength, but it would not move—it was frozen. She swung the ax against it again and again with all of her might until, finally, the ax handle turned in her weary hand and fell. She stood there exhausted and breathing heavily.

The bitter snow stung her face like heat—like the heat of the stove. What should she do? She knew it was important to keep her head and think. If she stayed there, the stove would go out. She turned and looked around. In the growing darkness she saw a man who stood with a rifle on his arm. He was looking at her.

"Garth! Oh, Garth!"

But even as the words left her lips, she knew it was not Garth.

She saw a man dressed in heavy furs, his face hidden in the hood he had drawn forward above his fur hat. He stood there silently, strangely still.

Then, suddenly, she remembered something. "The stove!" she said. "The stove!"

"What stove?"

"The stove. The stove—in our cabin. There's no more wood for the stove."

The man seemed not to understand. "The stove," she repeated, "there in the cabin. It's going out!"

Still he waited.

"There's a sick man there—my brother," she said finally. "Are you going to help me?"

She imagined, somehow, that he was laughing in the shadow of his hood. "But why should I help you?" he asked.

She had no more words. Silently she held out to him her bleeding hands.

After a long minute he stirred slowly. Without a word he placed his gun on two branches that grew above her reach. He lifted the ax from the snow, made a dozen sharp cuts, and watched the branch fall. Then, putting his foot on it, he chopped it quickly into four or five pieces. As each piece rolled free, Dorette grabbed it the way a starving woman might grab bread.

"That enough?"

She stared at him. "No, no!" she stammered. "It's not enough for the night. Cut me some more!"

She turned away and hurried toward the cabin. Halfway there he overtook her. Without a word he lifted the logs from her arms into his own. She was too tired to thank him. Without speaking she moved at his side, conscious only that help was here. She might yet save Derek.

In the cabin there was no light at all, no glow from the stove. Dorette swung open the door of the stove. She saw only a handful of gray-red ashes.

With trembling hands she grabbed a few twigs and threw them into the stove. The man who had followed her pushed her aside. She watched as he broke a few branches and coaxed them into flame. He tickled the appetite of the stove with some larger branches. Soon the fire took hold of the logs and fed upon them, hissing. He shut the door of the stove and turned to her.

She had lit a lamp and in the light stood looking at him. Her eyes were filled with gratitude.

"My brother's still living," she said, pointing to Derek in the bunk. The man's eyes did not follow the gesture as he said abruptly, "You stay here with him. I'm going to get more wood."

"You're a good man," she said. "I want to thank—"

But before she could finish speaking, he was at the door and out into the night.

He returned in half an hour, loaded down with wood. He did not speak to her, but busied himself feeding the stove. Then he picked up the ax and went out again. When he returned the second time, she was asleep.

Silent and untiring, he worked all night.

When she awoke the next morning, the man who had fed the stove all night was standing in the doorway. The door was open and there was a frosty freshness in the air. The world outside was bright with sun. A crow called in the forest. She looked at the stranger and said, "I did not mean to sleep. Why did you let me sleep while you worked?"

He said, almost roughly, "You were all tired out."

She said, "I knew you were a good man."

"Well," he answered slowly, "for one night."

His furred hood hid his face. She said, "Let me see you. Let me see your face."

"Why?"

She faltered, confused. She did not know why. "Because of what you have done—of what we owe you."

"We?"

"My brothers and I. Derek's still alive. I almost think he's sleeping better—more natural. When Garth comes home, he'll thank you too."

He had turned away from her again and was gazing down the trail. After a moment he said, "There's coffee on the back of the stove and some cornbread. You'd better eat. I've had some."

She had just reached the stove when he called, asking her to come to the door. When she joined him there, she saw again that strange look on his face that she had seen the night before.

He said quickly, "You're looking for your brother to come back?"

"Yes, yes. Any time."

"With another man?"

"With the doctor. Why?"

He raised his arm and pointed. In the glistening snow she saw two small, dark figures just rounding the curve in the trail.

Her heart was flooded with thankfulness. "Yes, yes, it's him and the doctor! Now you'll let him thank you."

Her words almost ended in a question, for she saw that he had his rifle on his arm and was putting on his snowshoes. Suddenly she felt uncomfortable. There was something in his silence, in his stillness, that was ominous and threatening.

She looked at him. In the shadow of the hood his eyes gleamed at her.

She breathed, "Who are you?"

"You'll know in a minute!"

He looked swiftly from her to the two men down the trail. They were coming on fast.

When they were so near that their faces could be seen, he quickly pushed her into the cabin. A bullet from the distance struck the snow near his feet. As a second bullet sent up a spray of dusty snow, the man raced into the forest and disappeared.

Dorette rushed to the door. She saw Garth down the trail, raising his rifle to fire again at the stranger.

"Get back!" shouted Garth. "That was Martin Dufour!"

When you read, it is important to be able to tell the difference between **fact and opinion**. A fact is a statement that is true. An opinion is a person's own feelings or views. Read the two sentences below. Which one is a fact? Which one is an opinion?

- Garth hated the outlaw Martin Dufour.
- Garth will probably capture Dufour one day.

Meet the Author

Marjorie Pickthall (1883–1922) was born in England, but she moved to Toronto, Canada, with her family when she was seven years old. Although Pickthall wrote poetry and novels, she is best known for her powerful short stories, many of which are set in the Canadian Northwest. "The Stove" is a good example of her writing. Pickthall, who loved the mountains and the woods, discovered that she wrote best when she was alone, surrounded by nature. She built a shack for herself under a huge pine tree. It was there that she did her writing.

CHECK YOUR READING

Put an **X** in the box next to the correct answer.

Reading Comprehension

1. Garth told Dorette that she had enough wood for
- ☐ **a.** three days.
- ☐ **b.** a week.
- ☐ **c.** ten days.

2. Derek was unable to move because he had
- ☐ **a.** broken his leg.
- ☐ **b.** hurt his back.
- ☐ **c.** been shot.

3. Dorette's main job was to
- ☐ **a.** get Derek to a doctor.
- ☐ **b.** keep the stove burning.
- ☐ **c.** keep the cabin neat.

4. Dorette was surprised that
- ☐ **a.** she had no more food.
- ☐ **b.** the woodpile was empty.
- ☐ **c.** it was very cold outside.

5. Dorette chopped up the chairs because she
- ☐ **a.** was very angry.
- ☐ **b.** needed the wood for the stove.
- ☐ **c.** didn't like them.

6. Who was the stranger who helped Dorette?
- ☐ **a.** one of Derek's friends
- ☐ **b.** the doctor
- ☐ **c.** Martin Dufour

Vocabulary

7. For miles around, there was nothing but the lonely and desolate forest. As used here, the word *desolate* means
- ☐ **a.** noisy.
- ☐ **b.** busy.
- ☐ **c.** empty.

8. Her brother's heart seemed to stop for a moment, but then it resumed its weak beating. The word *resumed* means
- ☐ **a.** began again.
- ☐ **b.** emptied out.
- ☐ **c.** listened to.

9. Now there were just a few logs on the floor. The large pile had diminished. The word *diminished* means
- ☐ **a.** became larger.
- ☐ **b.** became smaller.
- ☐ **c.** became better.

Idioms

10. As Dorette stood in the freezing cold, she realized that it was important to keep her head and think. When you *keep your head*, you
- ☐ **a.** remain calm.
- ☐ **b.** become frightened.
- ☐ **c.** shout for help.

UNDERSTANDING THE STORY

Exercise A ~ Checking Comprehension

Answer each question by writing a complete sentence. Be sure your sentences are grammatically correct. You may look back at the story.

1. When did Garth think he would return?

_____

2. How much food did Dorette have?

_____

3. Why was Garth going to Mandore?

_____

4. What had happened to Derek?

_____

5. What was the most important thing that Dorette could do for Derek?

_____

6. What did Dorette dream?

_____

7. Why was Dorette afraid to fall asleep?

_____

8. What did Dorette discover when she went to the woodpile?

_____

9. Why couldn't Dorette see the stranger's face?

_____

10. Where did the stranger go at the end of the story?

_____

Exercise B ~ Adding Vocabulary

In the box are 10 words from the story. Complete each sentence by adding the correct word.

restless	possessed	gratitude	witnessed	mocking
swayed	intolerable	thud	gems	wilderness

1. Dorette was used to hard work because she had been born in the

   _____ and had grown up there.

2. Although Dorette looked weak, she _____ a spirit of steel.

3. In her mind she saw the scene she had not _____.

4. The voice of the stove was at first annoying; then it became

   _____.

5. Everything was sparkling brilliantly as though made of

   _____.

6. She could hear the soft _____ of snow falling to the ground.

7. The load of logs was so heavy she _____ under its weight.

8. Dorette found it difficult to sleep, and spent a _____ night.

9. The loud screams of the stove seemed to be _____ Dorette.

10. When the stranger lit a fire in the stove, she was filled with

    _____.

Exercise C ~ Building Sentences by Using Connectives

Connectives are words that connect sentences smoothly and clearly. Usually, connectives appear at the beginning of a sentence, followed by a comma. Some common connectives are *therefore*, *however*, *finally*, *furthermore*, *thus*, *as a result*, and *moreover*. Connectives can add style and force to your writing.

Below are 10 pairs of sentences. Begin the second sentence in each pair with the connective in parentheses. Use capital letters and commas. Write both sentences on the line. The first one has been done for you.

1. Derek was very close to death. Garth hurried to get a doctor. (therefore)

   Derek was very close to death. Therefore, Garth hurried to get a doctor.

2. The men tracked Martin Dufour to a lonely little shack. Dufour managed to escape. (however)

3. The cold in that country kills like a sword. It was important to keep the cabin warm. (therefore)

4. There was no firewood in the cabin. There was a strong possibility that the fire in the stove would die out. (as a result)

5. Dorette had difficulty falling asleep. When she slept, she had bad dreams. (moreover)

73

6. It was hard for Dorette to chop the branch because it was frozen. Her hands were bloody and bruised. (furthermore)

_____

_____

_____

7. For a long time the stranger stared silently at Dorette. He decided to speak to her. (finally)

_____

_____

_____

8. Martin Dufour was the family's enemy. Dorette didn't realize that the stranger was Dufour. (however)

_____

_____

_____

9. The man threw some twigs and branches into the stove. They burst into flame. (finally)

_____

_____

_____

10. Dufour realized that Garth would arrive at the cabin soon. Dufour knew that he had to leave at once. (thus)

_____

_____

_____

Exercise D ~ Finding Synonyms

Read the sentence. Then select the **synonym** (the word most similar in meaning) for the word in capital letters. Put an **X** in the box next to the correct answer. Each capitalized word appears in the story.

1. "I hate to leave you," Garth said anxiously.
   ANXIOUSLY
   ☐ **a.** thoughtfully
   ☐ **b.** foolishly
   ☐ **c.** nervously

2. Dorette leaned over and kissed Derek's cheek, but Derek did not stir from his sleep.
   STIR
   ☐ **a.** move
   ☐ **b.** call
   ☐ **c.** dream

3. Dorette found a long stick and prodded the pile of logs.
   PRODDED
   ☐ **a.** pushed
   ☐ **b.** built
   ☐ **c.** leaped

4. The wood was hard and difficult to chop, but Dorette toiled on and did not stop.
   TOILED
   ☐ **a.** wished
   ☐ **b.** worked
   ☐ **c.** sang

5. It was like a savage beast striking out through the bars of its cage.
   SAVAGE
   ☐ **a.** wild
   ☐ **b.** gentle
   ☐ **c.** huge

6. Dorette's hands had been scorched by the door of the stove.
   SCORCHED
   ☐ **a.** scratched
   ☐ **b.** burned
   ☐ **c.** broken

7. She pleaded with Derek, "Take a mouthful of soup."
   PLEADED
   ☐ **a.** hoped
   ☐ **b.** forced
   ☐ **c.** begged

8. There was something in the stranger's silence that was frightening and ominous.
   OMINOUS
   ☐ **a.** pleasant
   ☐ **b.** surprising
   ☐ **c.** threatening

9. Dorette did not answer him immediately. She was confused and she faltered.
   FALTERED
   ☐ **a.** hesitated
   ☐ **b.** asked
   ☐ **c.** hurried

10. She moved without speaking, conscious only that help was near.
    CONSCIOUS
    ☐ **a.** asleep
    ☐ **b.** aware
    ☐ **c.** afraid

Exercise E ~ Understanding Characters and Plot

The following questions review **characters** and **plot** in the story. Put an **X** in the box next to the correct answer.

1. The main character in a story is the person the story is mostly about. Who is the main character in "The Stove"?

☐ **a.** Dorette

☐ **b.** Derek

☐ **c.** Martin Dufour

2. Which description best characterizes Dorette?

☐ **a.** She was lazy and hated to work.

☐ **b.** She was selfish and cared only about herself.

☐ **c.** She was a brave and determined person.

3. Select the statement that best characterizes Martin Dufour.

☐ **a.** He was a kind man who was loved by everyone.

☐ **b.** He was always friendly and helpful.

☐ **c.** He was a hated outlaw who did one good deed.

4. What happened first in the plot of "The Stove"?

☐ **a.** The stranger lit a fire in the stove.

☐ **b.** Garth headed down the trail toward Mandore.

☐ **c.** Dorette began to chop up some of the things in the cabin.

5. What happened last in the plot of the story?

☐ **a.** Garth fired a shot at Martin Dufour.

☐ **b.** The stranger chopped a branch into four or five pieces.

☐ **c.** Dorette stayed up all night to feed the stove.

6. Which one of the following events played the most important part in the plot of the story?

☐ **a.** Dorette discovered that the woodpile was empty.

☐ **b.** Dorette started to stitch a shirt she was making for Garth.

☐ **c.** Dorette ran down the trail and shouted, "Garth!"

Exercise F ~ Vocabulary Review

Write a complete sentence for each word.

1. desolate _____

_____

2. resumed _____

_____

3. gems _____

_____

4. restless _____

_____

5. gratitude _____

_____

6. intolerable _____

_____

7. toiled _____

_____

8. scorched _____

_____

9. ominous _____

_____

10. conscious _____

_____

STUDYING THE STORY

A. Looking Back at the Story

Discuss these questions with your partner or with the group. Your teacher may ask you to write your answer to one or more of the questions.

■ The stove itself may be viewed as a character in this story. Do you agree or disagree with this statement? Offer reasons to support your answer.

■ When Martin Dufour saw Dorette, he stood for a long time "silently, strangely still." What do you think might have been worrying Dufour? Why did he finally decide to help Dorette? Give several possible reasons.

■ Did you suspect that the stranger was Martin Dufour? If so, when did you first consider this possibility? What clues in the story suggest the stranger's identity?

■ Dorette told the stranger that he was "a good man." He responded by saying, "Well, for one night." What did each character mean? Who was right? Why?

B. Charting Similes in a Story

A **simile** compares two things by using the words *like* or *as*. For example, "Maria runs like a deer" is a simile. Similes help to "paint a picture in words" They make an author's writing vivid and descriptive. Fill in the chart below by completing some similes that appear in "The Stove." Look back at the story to find them. An example of a simile appears on the chart.

Similies That Appear in "The Stove"
1. The roar of the stove filled the cabin like ___*a hungry voice*___ .
2. The cold of that country kills like _____ .
3. "We'll follow and shoot him down like _____ ."
4. The fierce heat licked out at her each time like _____ .
5. The warmth was like _____ .
6. It was a world sparkling brilliantly as _____ .
7. The cold was creeping into the cabin in long fingers of frost that twisted like _____ .

THINKING ABOUT LITERATURE

1. Nature played a very important part in "The Stove." Find specific examples to support this statement. In your answer, demonstrate that Dorette had to struggle with a force of nature.

   Nature played a very important part in "The Stove."

   _____

   _____

   _____

   _____

   _____

   _____

   _____

2. Give three reasons that explain why the story is called "The Stove."

   a. _____

   _____

   b. _____

   _____

   c. _____

   _____

   On the line below, write another title for the story that would also be appropriate. Put the title in quotation marks.

   _____

3. Obviously, in "The Stove," there is **conflict** between Garth and Martin Dufour. At the beginning of the story, we learn how Garth and some men tracked down the outlaw. At the end of the story, Garth raises his rifle to fire at Dufour, who is racing away. On the lines below, write a scene in which Garth chases Dufour, who eventually escapes. Try to make your description as vivid as possible.

_____

_____

_____

_____

_____

_____

_____

_____

_____

_____

_____

_____

_____

4. Suppose that the stranger had *not* appeared. On the lines below, explain how you think the story might have ended.

_____

_____

_____

_____

_____

_____

_____

_____

_____

_____

_____

_____

_____

_____

_____

_____

UNIT 5
EARLY AUTUMN

BY LANGSTON HUGHES

GETTING READY TO READ

1. The Story and You

Years ago, Bill and Mary were in love. Then something "not very important" happened, and they drifted apart. As you will see in "Early Autumn," Mary still seems to have fond feelings for Bill. Sometimes, friends, relatives, acquaintances, teachers, and other people move out of your life. However, you may still care about them. Think of someone you have not seen for a long time and wonder about. Identify the person you chose and explain why that person is still meaningful to you.

2. Learning About Literature

As you know, **conflict** refers to a struggle, a fight, or a difference of opinion between characters. A character can also clash with a force of nature. Sometimes, however, a character experiences inner conflict. **Inner conflict** is a struggle that takes place in the *mind* of a character. When you read "Early Autumn," think about which character or characters faced inner conflict earlier and if either character is experiencing inner conflict now.

3. Looking Ahead

Look at the illustration on the left. Does the story take place in a city or in the country? How old do you think the two characters are? In your opinion, which character is older? Do you think that the man and the woman are married, friends, acquaintances, or strangers? Will the story probably be happy, sad, mysterious, or frightening? Read on to see if you are right.

EARLY AUTUMN

BY LANGSTON HUGHES

They were in love . . . a long time ago . . .

When Bill was very young, they had been in love. Many nights they had spent walking, talking together. Then something not very important had come between them, and they didn't speak. Impulsively, she had married a man she thought she loved. Bill went away, bitter about women.

Yesterday, walking across Washington Square,[1] she saw him for the first time in years.

"Bill Walker," she said.

He stopped. At first he did not recognize her, to him she looked so old.

"Mary! Where did you come from?"

Unconsciously, she lifted her face as though wanting a kiss, but he held out his hand. She took it.

"I live in New York now," she said.

"Oh"—smiling politely. Then a little frown came quickly between his eyes.

"Always wondered what happened to you, Bill."

"I'm a lawyer. Nice firm, way downtown."

"Married yet?"

"Sure. Two kids."

"Oh," she said.

A great many people went past them through the park. People they didn't know. It was late afternoon. Nearly sunset. Cold.

"And your husband?" he asked her.

"We have three children. I work in the bursar's office[2] at Columbia."

---

1. *Washington Square:* a park in Greenwich Village, a section of New York City

2. *bursar's office*: an office, usually at a college, that receives and pays bills

"You're looking very . . ." (he wanted to say old) ". . . well," he said.

She understood. Under the trees in Washington Square, she found herself desperately reaching back into the past. She had been older than he then in Ohio. Now she was not young at all. Bill was still young.

"We live on Central Park West," she said. "Come and see us sometime."

"Sure," he replied. "You and your husband must have dinner with my family some night. Any night. Lucille and I'd love to have you."

The leaves fell slowly from the trees in the Square. Fell without wind. Autumn dusk. She felt a little sick.

"We'd love it," she answered.

"You ought to see my kids." He grinned.

Suddenly the lights came on up the whole length of Fifth Avenue, chains of misty brilliance in the blue air.

"There's my bus," she said.

He held out his hand, "Good-bye."

"When . . ." she wanted to say, but the bus was ready to pull off.

The lights on the avenue blurred, twinkled, blurred. And she was afraid to open her mouth as she entered the bus. Afraid it would be impossible to utter a word.

Suddenly she shrieked very loudly, "Good-bye!" But the bus door had closed.

The bus started. People came between them outside, people crossing the street, people they didn't know. Space and people. She lost sight of Bill. Then she remembered she had forgotten to give him her address—or to ask him for his—or tell him that her youngest boy was named Bill, too.

Meet the Author

Langston Hughes (1902–1967) was born in Joplin, Missouri, and spent his early years in Lawrence, Kansas, and Cleveland, Ohio, where he graduated from high school. It was there that his first short stories were published in a monthly literary magazine. Hughes was only nineteen years old when he wrote the powerful poem "The Negro Speaks of Rivers." Five years later, after the publication of his first book, he received a scholarship to Lincoln University. After graduating, Hughes lived in Harlem, New York City, where he became a leading figure in literature and the arts. During his career Hughes wrote short stories, poems, songs, novels, plays, articles, movie scripts, and an autobiography. In all, he published more than fifty books. His poems have been translated into almost every language, and many have been set to music. They are sad, humorous, moving, and demonstrate a deep concern for humanity.

THE CITY

BY LANGSTON HUGHES

In the morning the city
Spreads its wings
Making a song
In stone that sings.

5   In the evening the city
Goes to bed
Hanging lights
Above its head.

LONELY HOUSE

BY LANGSTON HUGHES

At night when everything is quiet
This old house seems to breathe a sigh.
Sometimes I hear a neighbor snoring,
Sometimes I hear a baby cry,

5   Sometimes I hear a staircase creaking,
Sometimes a distant telephone.
Then the quiet settles down again,
The house and I are all alone.

Lonely house! Lonely me!
10 Funny with so many neighbors
How lonely it can be.

Oh, lonely street! Lonely town!
Funny you can be so lonely
With all these folks around.

15 I guess there must be something
I don't comprehend—
Sparrows have companions,
Even stray dogs find a friend.

The night for me is not romantic.
20 Unhook the stars and take them down.
I'm lonely in this lonely house
In this lonely town.

DECLARATION

BY LANGSTON HUGHES

If I was a sea-lion
Swimming in the sea,
I would swim to China
And you never would see me.
5   No!
       You never would
       See me.

If I was a rich boy
I'd buy myself a car,
10 Fill it up with gas
And drive so far, so far.
       Yes!
       I would drive
       So far.

15 Hard-hearted and unloving!
Hard-hearted and untrue!
If I was a bird I'd
Fly away from you.
       Yes, way
20   Away
       From
       You.

DREAMS

BY LANGSTON HUGHES

Hold fast to dreams
For if dreams die
Life is a broken-winged bird
That cannot fly.

5 Hold fast to dreams
For when dreams go
Life is a barren field
Frozen with snow.

CHECK YOUR READING

Put an **X** in the box next to the correct answer.

Reading Comprehension

1. Bill and Mary had not seen each other for
- ☐ **a.** several days.
- ☐ **b.** a few weeks.
- ☐ **c.** years.

2. Where does Mary live now?
- ☐ **a.** in Ohio
- ☐ **b.** in Washington
- ☐ **c.** in New York

3. What does Bill do for a living?
- ☐ **a.** He is a lawyer.
- ☐ **b.** He works at a college.
- ☐ **c.** The story does not give this information.

4. Which statement is true?
- ☐ **a.** Bill was older than Mary.
- ☐ **b.** Mary was older than Bill.
- ☐ **c.** Bill and Mary were about the same age.

5. Why couldn't Bill and Mary have dinner together one day?
- ☐ **a.** They did not exchange addresses.
- ☐ **b.** They were both too busy.
- ☐ **c.** Bill didn't invite Mary to dinner.

6. What was the name of one of Mary's children?
- ☐ **a.** Lucille
- ☐ **b.** Walker
- ☐ **c.** Bill

7. "Early Autumn" takes place
- ☐ **a.** in a park.
- ☐ **b.** on a bus.
- ☐ **c.** in an office.

Vocabulary

8. Bill said that he worked in a firm, way downtown. As used here, the word *firm* means
- ☐ **a.** very solid.
- ☐ **b.** building.
- ☐ **c.** a company.

9. Mary unconsciously lifted her face, as though wanting a kiss. When you do something *unconsciously*, you do it
- ☐ **a.** very slowly and carefully.
- ☐ **b.** without thinking about it.
- ☐ **c.** with much sorrow.

Idioms

10. Bill didn't realize that it was Mary, at first. The idiom *at first* means
- ☐ **a.** later.
- ☐ **b.** immediately.
- ☐ **c.** soon.

How many questions did you answer correctly? Circle your score. Then fill in your score on the Score Chart on page 184.

Number Correct	Score
1	10
2	20
3	30
4	40
5	50
6	60
7	70
8	80
9	90
10	100

Understanding the Story

Exercise A ~ Checking Comprehension

Answer each question by writing a complete sentence. Be sure your sentences are grammatically correct. You may look back at the story.

1. Why didn't Bill recognize Mary when she called to him?

_____

2. Where does Mary live now?

_____

3. What does Bill do for a living?

_____

4. How many children does Bill have?

_____

5. Where does Mary work?

_____

6. Who is older, Bill or Mary?

_____

7. At what time of the year does the story take place?

_____

8. Why was Mary afraid to open her mouth as she entered the bus?

_____

9. Why couldn't Bill and Mary have dinner together one day?

_____

10. What name had Mary given to her youngest son?

_____

Exercise B ～ Adding Punctuation

The following sentences need **punctuation marks**. Add capital letters, periods, commas, question marks, exclamation points, apostrophes, and quotation marks where necessary. Write the corrected sentences on the lines.

1. mary worked in the bursars office at columbia university

_____

_____

_____

2. she lived in ohio but then she moved to an apartment on central park west in new york city

_____

_____

_____

3. bill walker she shouted loudly at the man

_____

_____

_____

4. where did you come from mary he asked

_____

_____

_____

5. at first bill didnt recognize marys face because shed gotten quite old

_____

_____

_____

6. she said i always wondered what happened to you bill

_____

_____

_____

7. they had spent many nights walking talking going to the movies and eating dinner together

_____

_____

_____

8. bill the lawyer asked isnt washington square park beautiful in autumn

_____

_____

_____

9. bills eyes met hers as boys girls men and women rushed past them

_____

_____

_____

10. good-bye she exclaimed as she boarded the fifth avenue bus

_____

_____

_____

Exercise C ~ Finding Synonyms

Read the sentence. Then select the **synonym** (the word most similar in meaning) for the word in capital letters. Put an **X** in the box next to the correct answer. Each capitalized word appears in the story.

1. It was autumn and the leaves slowly dropped from the trees.

   AUTUMN
   - ☐ **a.** summer
   - ☐ **b.** winter
   - ☐ **c.** fall

2. It was difficult to see in the late afternoon dusk.

   DUSK
   - ☐ **a.** dark
   - ☐ **b.** dust
   - ☐ **c.** time

3. When the lights went on, they gave Fifth Avenue a certain brilliance.

   BRILLIANCE
   - ☐ **a.** brightness
   - ☐ **b.** motion
   - ☐ **c.** shadow

4. After Bill and Mary stopped speaking to each other, Bill went away feeling bitter about women.

   BITTER
   - ☐ **a.** glad
   - ☐ **b.** shocked
   - ☐ **c.** unpleasant

5. Since the air was misty, they could not see the bus very clearly.

   MISTY
   - ☐ **a.** hazy
   - ☐ **b.** cool
   - ☐ **c.** dry

6. Mary impulsively married a man she thought she loved.

   IMPULSIVELY
   - ☐ **a.** suddenly
   - ☐ **b.** sadly
   - ☐ **c.** thoughtfully

7. The lights on the avenue twinkled like stars.

   TWINKLED
   - ☐ **a.** fell
   - ☐ **b.** started
   - ☐ **c.** sparkled

8. Bill grinned and said, "You ought to see my kids."

   GRINNED
   - ☐ **a.** shook
   - ☐ **b.** shouted
   - ☐ **c.** smiled

9. Mary was afraid to open her mouth because she feared she would be unable to utter a word.

   UTTER
   - ☐ **a.** spell
   - ☐ **b.** say
   - ☐ **c.** need

10. Suddenly she shrieked very loudly, "Good-bye!"

    SHRIEKED
    - ☐ **a.** whispered
    - ☐ **b.** screamed
    - ☐ **c.** wondered

Exercise D ∼ Word Families

Fill in the blanks by writing the correct word from each family of words. Use each word once. The first one has been done for you.

despair	despaired	desperate	desperately	desperation

1. Mary *despaired* of ever seeing Bill again.

2. She _____ wanted to discuss what had happened years ago.

3. When they stopped seeing each other, he was filled with

_____.

4. His unusual behavior convinced his friends that he was a very

_____ man.

5. Calling every Bill Walker listed in the phone book was an act of

_____.

recognize	recognized	recognizing	recognizable	recognition

6. When Mary saw Bill, she _____ him at once.

7. She succeeded in _____ Bill, although she had not seen him for years.

8. For a moment, Bill did not _____ the woman who was calling his name.

9. Langston Hughes's poems and stories have earned him worldwide

_____.

10. Hughes has his own unique writing style. It is very

_____.

Exercise E ~ Thinking Critically

How well can you "read between the lines"? The following questions will help you think critically about the story you have just read. Put an **X** in the box next to the correct answer.

1. We may infer that Mary
☐ **a.** no longer cared about Bill.
☐ **b.** never cared about Bill.
☐ **c.** still cared about Bill very much.

2. We may conclude that Bill
☐ **a.** was still in love with Mary.
☐ **b.** no longer cared deeply about Mary.
☐ **c.** wanted very much to see Mary again.

3. Mary had "impulsively married a man she thought she loved." The author provides this information to suggest that Mary
☐ **a.** hated her husband.
☐ **b.** loved her husband very much.
☐ **c.** no longer loved her husband as much as she once thought she did.

4. Bill's attitude toward Mary is shown by the fact that he
☐ **a.** did not give her a kiss, but shook her hand.
☐ **b.** said that she looked very well.
☐ **c.** told her that he was a lawyer.

5. Bill and Mary will probably
☐ **a.** have dinner together some time.
☐ **b.** never have dinner together.
☐ **c.** become good friends.

6. The last sentence of the story suggests that Mary
☐ **a.** had a bad memory.
☐ **b.** was trying to forget about Bill.
☐ **c.** had loved Bill very much.

Exercise F ~ **Vocabulary Review**

Write a complete sentence for each word or idiom.

1. unconsciously _____

_____

2. misty _____

_____

3. dusk _____

_____

4. impulsively _____

_____

5. brilliance _____

_____

6. utter _____

_____

7. twinkled _____

_____

8. desperately _____

_____

9. recognition _____

_____

10. at first (idiom) _____

_____

STUDYING THE STORY

A. Looking Back at the Story
Discuss these questions with your partner or with the group. Your teacher may ask you to write your answer to one or more of the questions.

- What was Mary's reaction when she first saw Bill? What was Bill's reaction when he realized that the woman who was calling to him was Mary?

- When Bill asked Mary about her husband, she responded by saying, "We have three children. I work in the bursar's office at Columbia." Why do you think Mary didn't answer Bill's question directly? What does this suggest about Mary's relationship with her husband? What information in the first paragraph supports this view?

- What invitations did Bill and Mary exchange before they parted? Do you think Mary's invitation was sincere? Was Bill's? Explain your answers.

B. Using a Chart to Create a Time Line
Below are some events that occurred in the lives of Mary and Bill. Use the chart to put the events in the order in which they took place. Write the correct letter in the box. The first one has been done for you. You may look back at the story. When you have finished, you will have created a time line of events in the lives of characters. The first one has been done for you.

1	2	3	4	5	6	7	8
b							

- **a.** Mary married a man she thought she loved.
- **b.** Bill and Mary were in love and spent many hours walking and talking together.
- **c.** Mary and Bill exchanged invitations.
- **d.** Something happened to the relationship between Mary and Bill, and they stopped talking.
- **e.** Bill said that he was a lawyer and had two children.
- **f.** Mary entered the bus.
- **g.** Mary said that she worked in a bursar's office and lived on Central Park West.
- **h.** Mary met Bill in Washington Square Park.

THINKING ABOUT LITERATURE

1. Bill and Mary probably both experienced **inner conflict** when their relationship changed. Mary's chance meeting with Bill suggests that she still feels inner conflict about Bill. Support these statements by listing specific references from the story on the lines below.

_____

_____

_____

_____

_____

_____

_____

_____

_____

_____

_____

_____

_____

_____

2. Relationships sometimes change a great deal with the passing of time. Think about an occasion when you met someone you had not seen for a long time. On the lines below tell about that meeting. Conclude by stating whether you look forward to meeting that person again. If you prefer, write about a time when you returned to a place you had not seen for a long time—perhaps a country, school, or house you once lived in. Describe your reactions and give as many details as you can.

_____

_____

_____

_____

_____

_____

_____

_____

_____

_____

_____

_____

_____

_____

3. The City

a. **Stanzas** are lines in a poem that go together. "The City" contains two stanzas. How many lines are there in each stanza? Which lines in each stanza rhyme?

_____

_____

b. Stanza 1 describes the city as it awakens. To what does the poet compare the city? Explain the meaning of "a song in stone that sings."

_____

_____

c. Stanza 2 describes the city as it goes to bed. What lights hang above the city's head? Think of as many as you can.

_____

_____

4. Lonely House

a. Read the poem to yourself again. What mood or feeling does the poem create? How many times (including the title) does the word _lonely_ appear? In a sentence state what the poem says.

_____

_____

_____

b. In what ways are "The City" and "Lonely House" similar? How are they different?

_____

_____

5. Declaration

a. How many stanzas are there in "Declaration"? How many lines are there in each stanza? Which lines in each stanza rhyme?

_____

_____

b. Why is the poem titled "Declaration"? Does the speaker in "Declaration" remind you, in any way, of Bill in "Early Autumn"? If so, explain how.

_____

_____

_____

6. Dreams

a. How many stanzas are there in "Dreams"? How many lines are there in each stanza? Which lines in each stanza rhyme?

_____

_____

b. A **metaphor** compares two things without using the words *like* or *as*. "Life is a broken-winged bird" is a metaphor. Find another metaphor in the poem.

_____

c. As you know, a **simile** compares two things by using the words *like* or *as*. Change the metaphors in the poem to similes.

_____

_____

d. Langston Hughes has written hundreds of poems. "Dreams" is one of his most popular and best loved. Why do you think this poem is so popular?

_____

_____

AN OCCURRENCE AT OWL CREEK BRIDGE

BY AMBROSE BIERCE

GETTING READY TO READ

1. The Story and You

During the American Civil War (1861-1865), the North and the South were opposing forces. In some cases, members of the same family were on different sides and fought against each other. Suppose that you found yourself in this kind of situation. What are some ways you might handle it?

2. Learning About Literature

The **setting** is the time and place of the action of the story—*when* and *where* the action takes place. "An Occurrence at Owl Creek Bridge" takes place during the American Civil War, when the armies of the North and the South were enemies. The story is set on a bridge in northern Alabama. When you read the story, you will see why the setting is so important to the story.

3. Looking Ahead

Look at the illustration on the left. How can you tell that the story is about war? How do you know that the war took place a long time ago? Notice the noose, or rope with a loop, at the top of the picture. What does that suggest? Does the man in the center of the picture seem rich or poor? Why? Who do you think he might be? Do you think that the story will have a happy ending or a sad one? Read on to see if you are right.

An Occurrence at Owl Creek Bridge

---

by Ambrose Bierce

He was waiting to die . . .

Part 1

A man stood on a bridge in northern Alabama, looking down into the swift water twenty feet below. The man's hands were behind his back, his wrists tied together with a cord. There was a rope around his neck. It was attached to a wooden beam above his head.

The man was standing on some boards that served as a temporary platform. Also on the platform were the men who were going to hang him—soldiers of the Union Army.[1] A sergeant was directing two of the soldiers. A short distance away from them was a captain who stood silently, his arms folded. At each end of the bridge was a guard holding a rifle. The guard's job was to prevent anyone from coming onto the bridge.

The man who was about to be hanged was about thirty-five years of age. He was not wearing a uniform and, judging from his clothes, was quite wealthy. He was a handsome man whose long dark hair was combed straight back. It fell behind his ears to the collar of his well-fitting coat. He had a moustache and a pointed beard, and his large dark-gray eyes had a kindly expression. Clearly, this was no common killer.

The preparations were now complete. The two soldiers looked at the sergeant. The sergeant turned to the captain, saluted, and waited for the signal—the signal that would send the condemned man to his death.

---

1. *Union Army*: the army of the North during the American Civil War (1861–1865); the North and the South fought against each other.

The man glanced down at the swirling water of the stream below. A piece of drifting wood caught his attention. His eyes followed it as it bobbed up and down in the current. How slowly it seemed to move! What a sluggish stream!

The man closed his eyes and fixed his last thoughts on his wife and children. The water, sparkling brightly in the sun, had bothered him. And now, something new distracted him. It was a sound that he could neither understand nor ignore—a sharp, loud banging, like a hammer pounding. It had the same ringing sound. He wondered what it was and whether it was far away or near, for it seemed to be both. The sounds grew louder and stronger. They stabbed his ears like the jabs of a knife. He was afraid that he would scream. What he heard was the ticking of his watch.

He opened his eyes and again saw the water below him. "If I could free my hands," he thought, "I could pull off this noose and jump into the stream. By diving under the water, I could evade the bullets. I could swim swiftly to the shore, run into the woods, and get away to my home. My home, thank goodness, is still outside their lines. My wife and children are still far away from the enemy."

These thoughts flashed into the doomed man's brain. And as they did, the captain nodded to the sergeant and gave the signal.

Part 2

Peyton Farquhar was a wealthy farmer. He came from an old and highly respected Alabama family. Farquhar was a southerner who believed very strongly in the cause of the South. Certain things had happened that prevented him from joining the army and taking part in the fight against the North. Farquhar hated this, for he longed to be a soldier. Meanwhile, he did what he could and waited for an opportunity to serve the South. He was sure that the opportunity would come. Then he would do whatever he was asked, would be willing to face any danger.

One evening Farquhar and his wife were sitting on a bench near the entrance to his land. Just then a soldier dressed in gray rode up to the gate and asked for a drink of water. Mrs. Farquhar was happy to serve the soldier, for his gray uniform revealed that he was a soldier from the South. While she was getting the water, Farquhar approached the dusty horseman and inquired eagerly for news from the front.

The man shook his head and said, "Soldiers from the North are getting ready to advance. They have reached the Owl Creek bridge and are preparing to send soldiers and supplies over it. Their commander has issued an order, which has been posted everywhere. I saw the order. It warns everyone to stay away from the bridge. Anyone caught interfering with the bridge will be hanged."

"How far is it to the Owl Creek bridge?" asked Farquhar.

"About thirty miles."

"Are there many soldiers from the North on this side of the bridge?"

"There is just a small squad half a mile away. And there is one guard with a rifle at this end of the bridge."

"Suppose a man could get around the squad? Suppose he was able to overpower the guard," said Farquhar, smiling. "What could he do then? What could he accomplish?"

The soldier thought for a moment. "He could do much damage," he said. "He could destroy the bridge and prevent the North from advancing. I was there a month ago. I noticed that last winter's flood had thrown a great deal of driftwood against the wooden pier of the bridge. It is now very dry and would burn very quickly."

Farquhar smiled again, and at that moment his wife returned with the water, which the soldier drank. He thanked her politely, bowed to them both, then rode away. An hour later, when it was dark, he headed back in the direction from which he had come. The man was a spy—a spy *for the North*!

Part 3

As Peyton Farquhar fell straight down from the bridge, he lost consciousness and was as one already dead. He was awakened from this state—ages later, it seemed to him—by a sharp pain in his throat. He also felt as though he were choking. Pain seemed to shoot downward from his neck to every part of his body. He could not think, could only feel, and what he felt was torment.

And then, suddenly, he became aware that he was falling. All at once, the light around him flashed upward, and there was a loud splash. There was a roaring in his ears and everything was cold and dark.

Suddenly he could think again. He knew that the rope had broken and that he had fallen into the stream. The noose around his neck was choking him, but it kept the water from reaching his lungs. To die of hanging at the bottom of a river!—The idea seemed crazy, absurd to him. He opened his eyes and saw above him a gleam of light—but how distant it was, how far away. He was still sinking, for the light was getting fainter and fainter, until it was merely a glimmer. Then the light began to grow brighter and he knew that he was rising to the surface of the water. He regretted that because he knew that the soldiers would see him. "To be hanged and drowned," he thought, "that is not so bad. But I do not wish also to be shot. No, I will not be shot. That is not fair."

A sharp pain in his wrists told him that he was trying to free his hands. He was not even aware that he was trying to do that. It was as though someone else were involved in the struggle. Still, he tried with all his strength to get free. And then the cord fell away, his arms parted, and he floated upward. As the light grew brighter, he could see his hands. They tore at the noose around his neck. They ripped off the rope.

His neck ached horribly and his brain was on fire. His heart felt as though it were going to explode. But his hands pounded fiercely at the water, beating it downward, forcing him up to the surface. He felt his head emerge; it was now out of the water. His eyes were blinded by the sunlight. He took a huge breath and filled his lungs with air.

He was now in control of himself. He felt the water rippling against his face, heard the sound as the water splashed against him. He looked at the forest on the bank of the river. He saw the trees, saw them clearly, saw the leaves with the insects on them. He saw flies and gray spiders spinning their webs from twig to twig. He saw rainbow-colored dewdrops glistening on the blades of grass. A fish slid along beneath his eyes and he heard the rush of its body moving through the water.

He had come to the surface facing down the stream. He turned his head and saw the bridge. He saw the soldiers on the bridge, the captain, and the sergeant. He saw their dark shadows against the blue sky. They shouted and pointed at him. The captain had drawn his pistol, but he did not fire.

Suddenly he heard a sharp cracking sound and something struck the water a few inches away from his face. He heard a second shot and saw one of the guards, his rifle raised, a thin cloud of blue smoke rising from the mouth of the gun. The man in the water saw the eye of the guard gazing at him through the sights of the rifle. He saw that it was a gray eye, and he remembered having read that gray eyes were the sharpest, that all famous sharpshooters had them. Still, this one had missed.

A current had caught Farquhar and turned him halfway around. He was now looking toward the forest. Suddenly the sound of a high, clear voice rang out behind him. It traveled loudly and distinctly across the water.

Although he was no soldier, Farquhar knew the meaning of that command. His body turned cold as he heard those cruel words:

"Attention company! . . . Ready! . . . Aim! . . . *Fire!*"

Part 4

Farquhar dived—dived as deeply as he could. The water roared like thunder in his ears, but still he heard the dull sound of shots. He rose again to the surface, and as he did, shining bits of metal hit him on the face and hands.

Gasping for breath, he looked around and saw that he had drifted further down the stream, nearer to safety. The soldiers had almost finished reloading their rifles. They fired again, but did not hit him.

The hunted man saw all this over his shoulder. He was now swimming strongly, vigorously, with the current. Suddenly he felt himself whirling around and around, spinning like a top. The water, the forest, the faraway bridge, the men—all of them flew by his eyes in a blur. He was being whirled with such speed, he felt dizzy and sick. Then, suddenly, he was flung up onto the shore far away from his enemies. He was safe, but could hardly believe it. He dug his fingers into the sand and threw handfuls of it all over himself. He shouted with joy! He wept with delight!

He looked around at the trees near him on the shore. They seemed to him like giant garden plants. A strange, beautiful light shone through their branches; the breeze rustling through the leaves was like music to his ears. He would have liked to remain in that enchanted spot.

Shots in the branches high above his head caused him to change his mind at once. He quickly jumped to his feet, rushed further up the shore, and plunged into the forest.

All that day he traveled. The forest seemed interminable; it went on and on forever. Nowhere could he find a break in the woods, not even a path. He had not known that he lived in so wild a region. There was something strange in this discovery.

By nightfall he was aching, fatigued, and very hungry, but he had his heart set on seeing his wife and children, and that urged him on. At last he found a road that led in what he knew was the right direction. It was as wide and straight as a city street, yet there was no one on it. There were no houses anywhere. He did not even hear the barking of a dog.

His neck was in pain, and when he lifted his hand to it, he found that it was very sore. He knew that there must be a black circle where the rope had been tied around it. His eyes felt so swollen he could no longer close them. His tongue was hot and dry with thirst. He opened his mouth to let in some air. How soft the grass was on the path. He could no longer feel the road beneath his feet! Probably, even though he was suffering, he had fallen asleep while walking.

Now he sees another scene. He stands at the gate of his own house. Everything is just as he left it, bright and beautiful in the morning sunlight. He must have traveled the entire night. He pushes open the gate and walks up the wide white walk. He sees a flutter of female clothing and his wife, looking fresh and cool and sweet, comes down from the porch to meet him. At the bottom of the steps she stands waiting. Her face is smiling and filled with joy. Ah, how beautiful she is! He rushes forward with extended arms. As he is about to hug her, he feels a stunning blow on the back of his neck. A blinding white light blazes all around him. There is a loud, crashing sound—then all is darkness and silence!

Peyton Farquhar was dead. His body, with a broken neck, swung gently from side to side beneath the timbers of the Owl Creek bridge.

When you **make a prediction**, you guess about what is going to happen. Did you guess that the story was going to end happily or sadly? Did you predict correctly?

Meet the Author

Ambrose Bierce (1842–1914) lived a life as strange as many of the short stories he wrote. Bierce was born in a log cabin in Chester, Ohio, the tenth of thirteen children, all of whom had first names beginning with the letter A. Bierce did not get along with his family, and at the age of fifteen, he left home when he found a full-time job. After serving in the Civil War, which provided the background for many of his finest stories, Bierce moved to California, where he worked on newspapers and wrote short stories. He achieved fame—and became known as "Bitter Bierce"—for writing horrifying tales that had shocking and terrifying endings. In December 1913, Bierce left San Francisco for Mexico, where he disappeared. Nobody has ever discovered how or when he died.

CHECK YOUR READING

Put an **X** in the box next to the correct answer.

Reading Comprehension

1. How old was Peyton Farquhar?
- ☐ **a.** about twenty years old
- ☐ **b.** about thirty-five years old
- ☐ **c.** about fifty years old

2. The ringing sound that Farquhar heard was a
- ☐ **a.** hammer pounding.
- ☐ **b.** rifle firing.
- ☐ **c.** watch ticking.

3. Which statement is not true?
- ☐ **a.** Farquhar was a wealthy farmer.
- ☐ **b.** Farquhar came from an Alabama family.
- ☐ **c.** Farquhar believed in the cause of the North.

4. During the course of the story, Farquhar imagined that
- ☐ **a.** the rope broke.
- ☐ **b.** his friends saved his life.
- ☐ **c.** the soldiers decided to let him go.

5. At the end of the story, Farquhar
- ☐ **a.** was hanged and died.
- ☐ **b.** escaped and returned home.
- ☐ **c.** shot one of the soldiers.

Vocabulary

6. By diving under the water, he hoped to evade the bullets. The word *evade* means to
- ☐ **a.** feel.
- ☐ **b.** see clearly.
- ☐ **c.** get away from.

7. His gray uniform revealed that he was a soldier from the South. The word *revealed* means
- ☐ **a.** showed.
- ☐ **b.** helped.
- ☐ **c.** honored.

8. He was choking and his body was filled with torment. The word *torment* means
- ☐ **a.** interest.
- ☐ **b.** pain.
- ☐ **c.** information.

9. His head began to emerge; soon it was out of the water. The word *emerge* means to
- ☐ **a.** bleed.
- ☐ **b.** hurt.
- ☐ **c.** come up.

Idioms

10. Farquhar had his heart set on seeing his family. The idiom *to have one's heart set on* means to
- ☐ **a.** feel weak.
- ☐ **b.** want very much.
- ☐ **c.** worry about.

How many questions did you answer correctly? Circle your score. Then fill in your score on the Score Chart on page 184.

Number Correct	Score
1	10
2	20
3	30
4	40
5	50
6	60
7	70
8	80
9	90
10	100

UNDERSTANDING THE STORY

Exercise A ~ Checking Comprehension

Answer each question by writing a complete sentence. Be sure your sentences are grammatically correct. You may look back at the story.

1. Where was the bridge located?

   _____

2. What was the job of the guards who stood at each end of the bridge?

   _____

3. How old was the man who was about to be hanged?

   _____

4. What was the ringing sound that Farquhar heard?

   _____

5. According to the order, what would happen to anyone caught interfering with the bridge?

   _____

6. How far was it from Farquhar's land to the Owl Creek bridge?

   _____

7. How would destroying the bridge have helped the South?

   _____

8. Who was the soldier in gray who rode up to Farquhar's gate?

   _____

9. What did Farquhar think had happened to the rope?

   _____

10. Whom did Farquhar think he saw just before he died?

    _____

Exercise B ~ Adding Vocabulary

In the box are 10 words from the story. Complete each sentence by adding the correct word.

condemned	absurd	interfering	jabs	glimmer
sluggish	distracted	temporary	interminable	rustling

1. The stream moved slowly; it was a _____ stream.

2. His thoughts were interrupted by loud banging sounds that

_____ him.

3. The sounds stabbed his ears like the _____ of a knife.

4. The boards would soon be removed; they were only a

_____ platform.

5. The order was intended to discourage anyone from

_____ with the bridge.

6. To die of hanging at the bottom of a river seemed

_____ to him.

7. The light got fainter and fainter until it was only a

_____.

8. The forest seemed _____; it went on and on forever.

9. The breeze _____ through the leaves was like music to his ears.

10. A signal from the captain would send the _____ man to his death.

Exercise C ~ Building Sentences
Part A
Combine two **simple sentences** into one **complex sentence** by using the **subordinating conjunction** in parentheses. Put the conjunction in the middle of the sentence. Then write the complex sentence on the line. The first one has been done for you.

Common Subordinating Conjunctions

after	since	although	so that
because	until	if	while

1. Farquhar was going to be hanged. He had disobeyed the commander's order. (because)

    Farquhar was going to be hanged because he had disobeyed the commander's order.

2. The man's wrists were tied together with a cord. He was helpless. (so that)

    _____

    _____

3. Farquhar wanted to join the army. He longed to be a soldier. (since)

    _____

    _____

4. His wife gave the soldier some water. Farquhar spoke to the soldier. (while)

    _____

    _____

5. Farquhar hoped to escape. That was impossible. (although)

    _____

    _____

6. The soldiers couldn't see Farquhar. He ran into the forest. (after)

_____

_____

7. Farquhar swam with the current. He was thrown onto the shore. (until)

_____

_____

8. He would be able to get home safely. He could escape into the woods. (if)

_____

_____

Part B

Combine the **simple sentences** into **complex sentences** by using the
subordinating conjunctions in the box below. Put the correct conjunction
in the middle of each sentence. Then write the sentence on the line. Use
each conjunction once.

after	so that	until	while

1. He thought about his wife. He stood on the bridge.

_____

_____

2. Farquhar shouted with joy. He safely reached the shore.

_____

_____

3. He hid in the forest. The soldiers could not see him.

_____

_____

4. Farquhar didn't stop running. He came to the gate of his house.

_____

_____

Exercise D ~ Finding Synonyms

Read the sentence. Then select the **synonym** (the word most similar in meaning) for the word in capital letters. Put an **X** in the box next to the correct answer. Each capitalized word appears in the story.

1. Farquhar felt himself whirling around and around like a toy.

   WHIRLING
   - ☐ **a.** turning
   - ☐ **b.** jumping
   - ☐ **c.** dancing

2. At the end of the day he was aching, fatigued, and very hungry.

   FATIGUED
   - ☐ **a.** bored
   - ☐ **b.** tired
   - ☐ **c.** amused

3. Farquhar saw a gray eye gazing at him.

   GAZING
   - ☐ **a.** looking
   - ☐ **b.** closing
   - ☐ **c.** remembering

4. The sound traveled loudly and distinctly across the water.

   DISTINCTLY
   - ☐ **a.** calmly
   - ☐ **b.** quickly
   - ☐ **c.** clearly

5. Farquhar approached the man and inquired whether he had any news.

   INQUIRED
   - ☐ **a.** paid
   - ☐ **b.** read
   - ☐ **c.** asked

6. What could a man accomplish if he were able to overpower the guard?

   ACCOMPLISH
   - ☐ **a.** do
   - ☐ **b.** want
   - ☐ **c.** steal

7. A blinding white light blazes all around him.

   BLAZES
   - ☐ **a.** opens
   - ☐ **b.** glows
   - ☐ **c.** ends

8. Farquhar jumped up quickly and plunged into the forest.

   PLUNGED
   - ☐ **a.** fell
   - ☐ **b.** searched
   - ☐ **c.** rushed

9. He looked down at the swirling waters of the stream.

   SWIRLING
   - ☐ **a.** empty
   - ☐ **b.** twisting
   - ☐ **c.** warm

10. Farquhar saw giant plants in that strange and wonderful enchanted place.

    ENCHANTED
    - ☐ **a.** dull
    - ☐ **b.** foolish
    - ☐ **c.** magical

Exercise E ~ Thinking Critically

How well did you understand "An Occurrence at Owl Creek Bridge"? This story, more than most, requires the reader to think critically. Put an **X** in the box next to the correct answer.

1. We may infer that Peyton Farquhar was hanged because he
- ☐ **a.** was a spy for the South.
- ☐ **b.** refused to help the North.
- ☐ **c.** was caught attempting to destroy the Owl Creek bridge.

2. Where does most of the action of the story take place?
- ☐ **a.** in Peyton Farquhar's mind
- ☐ **b.** on a battlefield
- ☐ **c.** in a forest

3. The main action of the story takes place over
- ☐ **a.** a few seconds.
- ☐ **b.** several weeks.
- ☐ **c.** a few months.

4. We may infer that Peyton Farquhar died thinking about
- ☐ **a.** his children.
- ☐ **b.** his wife.
- ☐ **c.** the spy who told him about the bridge.

5. Immediately before Farquhar died, he
- ☐ **a.** almost escaped.
- ☐ **b.** shouted at the soldiers.
- ☐ **c.** began to dream.

6. "An Occurrence at Owl Creek Bridge" is different from most stories because it
- ☐ **a.** has no main character.
- ☐ **b.** is very short.
- ☐ **c.** moves back and forth in time.

Exercise F ~ Vocabulary Review

Write a complete sentence for each word or idiom.

1. evade _____

_____

2. revealed _____

_____

3. emerge _____

_____

4. sluggish _____

_____

5. absurd _____

_____

6. interfering _____

_____

7. temporary _____

_____

8. accomplish _____

_____

9. interminable _____

_____

10. have his (or her) heart set on (idiom)_____

_____

STUDYING THE STORY

A. Looking Back at the Story

Discuss these questions with your partner or with the group. Your teacher may ask you to write your answer to one or more of the questions.

- Ambrose Bierce is famous for writing surprising and shocking tales. "An Occurrence at Owl Creek Bridge" is a good example of his work. In what ways is this selection different from most stories you have read? Give several reasons.

- Read the last sentence in Part 1. Then read the last sentence of the story again. How much time takes place between these two sentences? The physical setting of the story is a bridge, but where does most of the action of the story really take place?

- At some point while reading the story, did you think that Peyton Farquhar had escaped, or were you aware all along that he had never really left the bridge? Explain.

- Were you disappointed that Farquhar did not escape? Why? If he had escaped, do you think this would have weakened the story, or would it have made it stronger? Explain.

B. Charting Character Traits

A character in a story might be courageous, friendly, foolish, or wise. These are **character traits** that describe the character. Complete the chart below by filling in four character traits for Peyton Farquhar. Add facts to support the character traits you chose.

| Peyton Farquhar | |
Character Traits	Supporting Facts

THINKING ABOUT LITERATURE

1. A **flashback** interrupts the action of the plot to show an event or events that occurred at an earlier time.

   a. Which part of "An Occurrence at Owl Creek Bridge" is a flashback?

   _____

   _____

   b. Refer to the selection to explain how a flashback can add interest and power to a story.

   _____

   _____

   _____

   _____

2. Do you think that Farquhar's dream made it easier for him to face death? Why?

   _____

   _____

   _____

   _____

3. Explain how the description of Farquhar's wife immediately before he died makes his death sadder and more shocking.

   _____

   _____

   _____

   _____

4. On the lines below, describe how Peyton Farquhar attempted to burn down the Owl Creek bridge and was caught. Use your imagination to make the description of the incident as vivid and as exciting as possible.

_____

_____

_____

_____

_____

_____

_____

_____

_____

_____

5. Suppose there were a Part 5 of "An Occurrence at Owl Creek Bridge." What do you think would happen? Think about how the story might continue. Then write the opening paragraph of that section.

_____

_____

_____

_____

_____

_____

_____

_____

_____

_____

UNIT 7
TA-NA-E-KA

BY MARY WHITEBIRD

GETTING READY TO READ

1. The Story and You

Grandpa Amos Deer Leg thought that young people should undertake Ta-Na-E-Ka, a kind of "test of survival" to prove that they were ready for adulthood. The test included living alone in the woods for five days without food and living on insects. Today, few people will experience something like Ta-Na-E-Ka. However, how are you preparing yourself to deal with the challenges of life that lie ahead? You might want to discuss plans for your education, your job experiences, and special skills that you are developing. Perhaps you are involved in activities that will assist you in the future.

2. Learning About Literature

In literature, the **narrator** is the person who tells the story. Usually, the narrator is the writer or a character in the story. In "Ta-Na-E-Ka," you will read about Mary, Roger, and their grandfather, Amos Deer Leg. See if one of these characters is the narrator of the story.

3. Looking Ahead

Look at the illustration on the left. Notice that the title of the story is "Ta-Na-E-Ka." That is a Kaw Indian word that means "flowering of adulthood." This suggests that the story has something to do with becoming an adult. Look at the girl in the center of the picture. How old do you think she is? What is she wearing? Do you think she speaks English or Kaw? Why do you think so? Do you think the action of the story takes place indoors or outside? Why? Notice that there is a hamburger in the illustration. How might that be important in the story? Read on to see if you are right.

Ta-Na-E-Ka

by Mary Whitebird

Only the strongest and smartest could survive . . .

My birthday was approaching and I had awful nightmares about it. I was reaching the age at which all Kaw Indians had to participate in Ta-Na-E-Ka. Well, perhaps not all Kaws. Some of the younger families on the reservation were beginning to give up the old customs. But my grandfather, Amos Deer Leg, was devoted to tradition. He still wore handmade beaded moccasins instead of shoes, and kept his iron gray hair in tight braids. He could speak English, but he spoke it only with white men. With his family he used a Sioux dialect.

Grandfather was one of the last living Indians (he died when he was 81) who actually fought against the U.S. Cavalry. At the time, my grandfather was only eleven years old.

Eleven was a magic word among the Kaws. It was the time of Ta-Na-E-Ka, the "flowering of adulthood." It was the age, my grandfather informed us hundreds of times, "when a boy could prove himself to be a warrior and a girl took the first steps to womanhood."

"I don't want to be a warrior," my cousin, Roger Deer Leg, confided to me. "I'm going to become an accountant."

"None of the other tribes make girls go through the endurance ritual,"[1] I complained to my mother.

"It won't be as bad as you think, Mary," my mother said, ignoring my protests. "Once you've gone through it, you'll certainly never forget it. You'll be proud."

I even complained to my teacher, Mrs. Richardson. I thought that, as a white woman, she would take my side.

She didn't. "All of us have customs of one kind or another," Mrs. Richardson said. "And look at it this way: How many girls have the

---

1. *endurance ritual*: a test to see how strong one is

opportunity to compete on equal terms with boys? Don't look down on your heritage."

Heritage, indeed! I had no intention of living on a reservation for the rest of my life!

But I was impressed with the way the Kaw treated women. No other Indian tribe treated women more "equally" than the Kaw. Unlike most of the tribes of the Sioux Nation, the Kaw allowed men and women to eat together. And even hundreds of years ago, a Kaw woman had the right to refuse to marry the man her father had chosen to be her husband.

The wisest women (generally the oldest) often sat in tribal councils. And most Kaw legends were about "Good Woman," a kind of superwoman who led Kaw warriors into battle after battle from which they always seemed to emerge victorious.

Girls as well as boys were required to go through Ta-Na-E-Ka. The ceremony varied from tribe to tribe, but since the Indians' life on the plains was one of survival, Ta-Na-E-Ka was a test of survival.

"Endurance is the greatest virtue of the Indian," my grandfather explained. "To survive, we must endure. When I was a boy," he went on, "Ta-Na-E-Ka was harder than it is now. We were painted white with the juice of a sacred herb and were sent naked into the wilderness without even a knife. We couldn't return until the white had worn off. It wouldn't wash off! It took almost eighteen days. During that time we had to stay alive—trapping food, eating insects and roots and berries, and watching out for enemies. And we did have enemies—the white soldiers and the Omaha[2] warriors, who were always trying to capture Kaw boys and girls undergoing their endurance test. It was an exciting time."

"What happened if you couldn't make it?" Roger asked. He was born only three days after I was, and we were being trained for Ta-Na-E-Ka together. I was happy to know he was frightened too.

---

2. *Omaha*: a Native American tribe that lived in northeastern Nebraska

"Many didn't return," Grandfather said. "Only the strongest and smartest made it. Mothers were not allowed to weep over those who didn't return. If a Kaw couldn't survive, he or she wasn't worth weeping over. It was our way."

"What a lot of hooey,"[3] Roger whispered. "I'd give anything to get out of it."

"I don't think we have any choice," I replied.

Roger gave my arm a little squeeze. "Well, it's only five days."

Five days! Maybe it was better than being painted white and sent out naked for eighteen days. But not much better.

We were to be sent, barefoot and in bathing suits, into the woods. For five days we'd have to live off the land, keeping warm as best we could, getting food where we could. It was May, but the days were still chilly and the nights were fiercely cold.

Grandfather was in charge of the month's training for Ta-Na-E-Ka. One day he caught a grasshopper and demonstrated how to pull its legs and wings off in one flick of the fingers and how to swallow it.

I felt sick, and Roger turned green. I told Roger teasingly, "You'd make a terrible warrior." Roger just made a face.

I knew one thing. I wasn't going to swallow a grasshopper no matter how hungry I got. And then I had an idea. Why hadn't I thought of it before? I would have saved nights of bad dreams about eating grasshoppers.

I headed straight for my teacher's house. "Mrs. Richardson," I said, "would you lend me five dollars?"

"Five dollars!" she exclaimed. "What for?"

"You remember the ceremony I talked about?"

"Ta-Na-E-Ka. Of course. Your parents have written me and asked me to excuse you from school so you can participate in it."

"Well, I need some things for the ceremony," I replied, in a half-truth. "I don't want to ask my parents for the money."

"It's not a crime to borrow money, Mary. But how can you pay it back?"

"I'll baby-sit for you."

"That's fair," she said, going to her purse and handing me a crisp, new, five-dollar bill. I'd never had that much money at once.

"I'm happy to know the money's going to be put to a good use," Mrs. Richardson said.

---

3. *hooey*: nonsense

A few days later, Ta-Na-E-Ka began. It started with a long speech from my grandfather about how we had reached the age of decision, how we now had to prove that we could take care of ourselves and survive. All the friends and relatives who had gathered at our house for dinner made jokes about their own Ta-Na-E-Ka experiences. They all advised us to eat well now, since for the next five days we'd be dining on crickets. Neither Roger nor I was very hungry. "I'll probably laugh about this when I'm an accountant," Roger said, trembling.

"Are you trembling?" I asked.

"What do you think?"

"I'm happy to know boys tremble too," I said.

At six the next morning we kissed our parents and went off to the woods. "Which side do you want?" Roger asked. According to the rules, Roger and I would each have our own "territories" in separate areas of the woods, and we weren't allowed to communicate with each other.

"I'll go toward the river, if it's okay with you," I said.

"Sure," Roger answered. "What difference does it make?"

To me, it made a lot of difference. There was a marina[4] a few miles up the river and there were some boats there. At least, I hoped so. I figured that I'd rather sleep in a boat than under a pile of leaves.

As we came to a fork in the trail, Roger shook my hand. "Good luck, Mary."

"N'ko-n'ta," I said. It was the Kaw word for *courage*.

The sun was shining and it was warm, but my bare feet began to hurt immediately. I spied one of the berry bushes Grandfather had told us about. "You're lucky," he had said. "The berries are ripe in the spring, and they are delicious and nourishing." They were orange and fat and I popped one into my mouth.

---

4. *marina*: a dock for boats

Argh! I spat it out. It was awful and bitter, and even grasshoppers probably tasted better, although I never intended to find out.

I sat down to rest my feet. A rabbit hopped out from under the berry bush. He poked the berry with his nose, then ate it. He picked another one and ate that too. He liked them. He looked at me while he twitched his nose. I watched a redheaded woodpecker tapping at an elm tree, and I caught a glimpse of a raccoon scampering through some twigs. All of a sudden I realized I was no longer frightened. Ta-Na-E-Ka might be more fun than I'd anticipated. I got up and headed toward the marina.

"Not one boat," I said to myself dejectedly. But the restaurant on the shore, "Ernie's Riverside," was open. I walked in, feeling silly in my bathing suit. The man at the counter was big and tough-looking. He wore a sweatshirt with the words "Fort Sheridan" on it. He asked me what I wanted.

"A hamburger and a milk shake," I said, holding the five-dollar bill in my hand so he'd know I had money.

"That's a pretty heavy breakfast," he murmured.

"That's what I always have for breakfast," I lied.

"Forty-five cents," he said, bringing me the food. (Back then, hamburgers were twenty-five cents and milk shakes were twenty cents.) "Delicious," I thought. "Better than grasshoppers—and Grandfather never once mentioned that I couldn't eat hamburgers!"

While I was eating, I had a terrific idea. Why not sleep in the restaurant? I went to the ladies' room and made sure that the window was unlocked. Then I went back outside and played along the riverbank. I watched the water birds and tried to identify each one. I planned to look for a beaver dam the next day.

The restaurant closed at sunset, and I watched the man drive away. Then I climbed in the unlocked window. There was a night light on, so I didn't turn on any lights. But there was a radio on the counter. I turned it on to a music program. It was warm in the restaurant, and I was hungry. I helped myself to a glass of milk and a piece of pie, intending to keep a list of what I'd eaten so I could leave money. I also planned to get up early, sneak out through the window, and head for the woods before the man returned. I turned off the radio, wrapped myself in the man's apron, and in spite of the hardness of the floor, fell asleep.

"What are you doing here, kid?"

It was the man's voice.

It was morning. I'd overslept. I was scared.

"Hold it, kid. I just want to know what you're doing here. You lost? You must be from the reservation. Your folks must be worried sick about you. Do they have a phone?"

"Yes, yes," I answered. "But don't call them."

I was shivering. The man, who told me his name was Ernie, made me a cup of hot chocolate while I explained about Ta-Na-E-Ka.

"Most amazing thing I ever heard," he said, when I was through. "I've lived next to the reservation all my life and this is the first I've heard of Ta-Na whatever-you-call-it." He looked at me, "Pretty silly thing to do to a kid," he muttered.

That was what I'd been thinking for months. But when Ernie said it, I became angry. "No, it *isn't* silly. It's a custom of the Kaw. We've been doing this for hundreds of years. My mother and my grandfather and everybody in my family went through this ceremony. It's why the Kaw are great warriors."

"Okay, great warrior," Ernie chuckled, "suit yourself. And, if you want to stick around, it's okay with me." Ernie went to the broom closet and tossed me a bundle. "That's the lost-and-found closet," he said. People leave stuff on boats. Maybe you'll find something to keep you warm."

The sweater fitted loosely, but it felt good. I felt good. And I'd found a new friend. Most important, I was surviving Ta-Na-E-ka.

My grandfather had said the experience would be filled with adventure, and I was having my fill. And Grandfather never said we couldn't accept hospitality.

I stayed at Ernie's Riverside for the entire period. In the mornings I went into the woods and watched the animals and picked flowers for each of the tables in Ernie's. I had never felt better. I was up early enough to watch the sun rise on the Missouri, and I went to bed after it set. I ate everything I wanted—insisting that Ernie take all my money for the food. "I'll keep this in trust for you, Mary," Ernie promised, "in case you are ever desperate for five dollars."

I was sorry when the five days were over. I'd enjoyed every minute with Ernie. He taught me how to make western omelets and how to make Chili Ernie Style (still one of my favorite dishes). And I told Ernie all about the legends of the Kaw. I hadn't realized I knew so much about my people.

Ta-Na-E-Ka was over, and as I approached my house, at about nine-thirty in the evening, I became nervous all over again. What if Grandfather asked me about the berries and the grasshoppers? And my feet were hardly cut. I hadn't lost a pound and my hair was combed.

"They'll be so happy to see me," I told myself hopefully, "that they won't ask too many questions."

I opened the door. My grandfather was in the front room. He was wearing the beaded deerskin shirt which had belonged to *his* grandfather. "N'g'da'ma," he said. "Welcome back."

I embraced my parents warmly. I let go only when I saw my cousin Roger sprawled on the couch. His eyes were red and swollen. He'd lost weight. His feet were red and covered with blisters, and he was moaning, "I made it, see. I made it. I'm a warrior! A warrior!"

My grandfather looked at me strangely. I was clean, obviously well fed, and very healthy. My parents got the message. My uncle and aunt gazed at me.

Finally my grandfather asked, "What did you eat to keep you so well?"

I sucked in my breath and blurted out the truth, "Hamburgers and milk shakes."

"Hamburgers!" my grandfather growled.

"Milk shakes!" Roger moaned.

"You didn't say we *had* to eat grasshoppers," I said quietly, a little embarrassed.

"Tell us about your Ta-Na-E-Ka," my grandfather commanded.

I told them everything, from borrowing the five dollars, to Ernie's kindness.

"That's not what I trained you for," my grandfather said sadly.

I stood up. "Grandfather, I learned that Ta-Na-E-Ka *is* important. I didn't think so during training. I was scared stiff of it. I handled it my way. And I learned I had nothing to be afraid of. There's no reason today to eat grasshoppers when you can eat a hamburger."

I was shocked at my own boldness. But I liked it. "Grandfather, I'll bet you never ate one of those rotten berries yourself."

Grandfather laughed! He laughed aloud! My mother and father

and aunt and uncle were all amazed. Grandfather never laughed!
Never!

"Those berries—they are terrible," Grandfather admitted. "I could never swallow them. I found a dead deer on the first day of my Ta-Na-E-Ka—shot by a soldier, probably—and that kept my belly full for the entire period of the test!"

Grandfather stopped laughing. "We should send you out again," he said.

I looked at Roger. "You're pretty smart, Mary," Roger groaned. "I'd never have thought of what you did."

Roger tried to smile, but couldn't. My grandfather called me to him.

"You should have done what your cousin did," he said. "But I think you are more alert to what is happening to our people today than we are. I think you would have passed the test in any time. Somehow, you know how to exist in a world that wasn't made for Indians. I don't think you're going to have any trouble surviving."

Grandfather wasn't entirely right. But I'll tell about that another time.

The **narrator** is the person who tells the story. Who is the narrator in "Ta-Na-E-Ka"?

Meet the Kaw

The Kaw, or Kansa Indians, lived west of the Mississippi River in what is now Kansas. In fact, both the state and the Kansas River take their name from Kansa, which means "people of the south wind." A proud people, who grew their own food and hunted buffalo, the Kaw were deeply devoted to family tradition, as "Ta-Na-E-Ka" suggests. As a result of smallpox and other diseases, their number has decreased over the years. Today most of the tribe lives in a small area in Osage County, Oklahoma, near Kansas. A celebrated Kaw tribal member was Charles Curtis, who served as vice president of the United States from 1929–1933. During his long career in Congress, he helped pass the Citizenship Act of 1924, which gave the right of United States citizenship to Native Americans.

GRANDFATHER

BY JAMES K. CAZALAS

It puzzles me
That I cannot see
What grandfather can:
He is eighty with the eyes
5   Of a young Indian
Proving his manhood.

I stumbled in the deep yellow sand
And he walked over it easily.
I breathed hard and perspired
10 And he paced himself
Like an animal
With a long way to go.

A dollar-sized turtle
Struggling on its back
15 Was dying ten feet off the sand:
It was he who saw it
And turned it over.

When we returned home,
He took off his sneakers,
20 Took out his teeth,
And was an old, dying man.
But on the trail
He was Seneca[1]
And more a part of the earth
25 Than the sand we trod.

---

1. *Seneca*: one of the five American Indian tribes that formed the powerful
   Iroquois nation

CHECK YOUR READING

Put an **X** in the box next to the correct answer.

Reading Comprehension

1. Kaw Indians took part in Ta-Na-E-Ka when they were
- ☐ **a.** ten years old.
- ☐ **b.** eleven years old.
- ☐ **c.** fifteen years old.

2. Roger wanted to become
- ☐ **a.** a great warrior.
- ☐ **b.** a teacher.
- ☐ **c.** an accountant.

3. Who was in charge of the training for Ta-Na-E-Ka?
- ☐ **a.** Mary's mother
- ☐ **b.** Mary's grandmother
- ☐ **c.** Mary's grandfather

4. How much money did Mary borrow from Mrs. Richardson?
- ☐ **a.** five dollars
- ☐ **b.** fifteen dollars
- ☐ **c.** twenty-five dollars

5. Where did Mary sleep during her Ta-Na-E-Ka?
- ☐ **a.** in a boat
- ☐ **b.** in a restaurant
- ☐ **c.** in a forest

6. When Mary returned home after her Ta-Na-E-Ka, she looked
- ☐ **a.** tired and thin.
- ☐ **b.** sick and bruised.
- ☐ **c.** clean and well fed.

Vocabulary

7. "I don't want to be a warrior," Roger confided to Mary. The word *confided* means
- ☐ **a.** told in secret.
- ☐ **b.** wished for greatly.
- ☐ **c.** walked away from.

8. When she returned home, Mary embraced her parents warmly. As used here, the word *embraced* means
- ☐ **a.** warned.
- ☐ **b.** hugged.
- ☐ **c.** noticed.

9. Grandfather thought that Mary was alert to what was happening to their people. As used here, the word *alert* means
- ☐ **a.** very aware.
- ☐ **b.** not concerned about.
- ☐ **c.** delighted with.

Idioms

10. When Mary complained about Ta-Na-E-Ka, she thought that Mrs. Richardson would take her side. When you *take someone's side*, you
- ☐ **a.** argue with that person.
- ☐ **b.** agree with that person.
- ☐ **c.** hit that person in the side.

How many questions did you answer correctly? Circle your score. Then fill in your score on the Score Chart on page 184.

Number Correct	Score
1	10
2	20
3	30
4	40
5	50
6	60
7	70
8	80
9	90
10	100

UNDERSTANDING THE STORY

Exercise A ~ Checking Comprehension

Answer each question by writing a complete sentence. Be sure your sentences are grammatically correct. You may look back at the story.

1. At what age were Kaw Indians supposed to participate in Ta-Na-E-Ka?

_____

2. What was Roger planning to be?

_____

3. What impressed Mary about the Kaw?

_____

4. How many days did Mary and Roger have to participate in Ta-Na-E-Ka?

_____

5. Who was in charge of the training for Ta-Na-E-Ka?

_____

6. How much money did Mrs. Richardson give Mary?

_____

7. What did Mary eat for breakfast on her first day of Ta-Na-E-Ka?

_____

8. Where did Mary stay during her entire Ta-Na-E-Ka?

_____

9. How did Mary look when she returned home?

_____

10. What did Grandfather eat during his Ta-Na-E-Ka?

_____

Exercise B ~ Adding Vocabulary

In the box are 10 words from the story. Complete each sentence by adding the correct word.

nourishing	survival	participate	dialect	intention
heritage	nightmares	hospitality	sprawled	protests

1. Ta-Na-E-Ka was the Kaw test of _____.

2. As Mary's birthday approached, she began to have awful

_____ about it.

3. Although Grandfather spoke English, he used a Sioux

_____ when he was with his family.

4. Mary had no _____ of remaining on the reservation
for the rest of her life.

5. Although Mary complained, Mary's mother ignored her

_____ .

6. Mrs. Richardson told Mary not to "look down" on her

_____ .

7. Mary was nervous about it, but she knew that she would have to

_____ in Ta-Na-E-Ka.

8. Grandfather said that berries tasted good and were very

_____ .

9. Mary accepted Ernie's _____ and stayed at the
restaurant.

10. There, _____ on the couch, was her cousin, Roger.

Exercise C ~ Combining Sentences Using Adjective Clauses

An **adjective clause** is a **subordinate clause** used as an adjective to modify a noun or a pronoun. Adjective clauses often begin with the **relative pronouns** *who, whom, which,* and *that.*

Combine each pair of sentences into one sentence that contains an adjective clause. Use the pronoun in parentheses. Write the sentence on the lines. The first one has been done for you.

1. Amos Deer Leg was a Kaw. He believed in tradition. (who)

Amos Deer Leg was a Kaw who believed in tradition.

2. Roger was an eleven-year-old boy. He wanted to be an accountant. (who)

_____

_____

3. Mary Whitebird was the author. She wrote "Ta-Na-E-Ka." (who)

_____

_____

4. Mrs. Richardson was a teacher. Everyone admired her. (whom)

_____

_____

5. She gave her a five-dollar bill. It was new and crisp. (that)

_____

_____

6. Roger ate berries. He found them on the bushes. (that)

_____

_____

7. Ernie gave Mary a sweater. It fitted loosely. (that)

_____

_____

8. Mary looked at Roger's eyes. They were red and swollen. (which)

_____

_____

9. She ate hamburgers. They were delicious. (which)

_____

_____

10. Grandfather wore beaded moccasins. They were beautiful. (which)

_____

_____

Exercise D ～ Finding Synonyms

Read the sentence. Then select the **synonym** (the word most similar in meaning) for the word in capital letters. Put an **X** in the box next to the correct answer. Each capitalized word appears in the story.

1. Ta-Na-E-Ka was a test of endurance.

   ENDURANCE
   - ☐ **a.** speed
   - ☐ **b.** strength
   - ☐ **c.** beauty

2. Only the strongest and smartest managed to survive.

   SURVIVE
   - ☐ **a.** live
   - ☐ **b.** help
   - ☐ **c.** complain

3. Mothers were not allowed to weep over a child who did not return.

   WEEP
   - ☐ **a.** cry
   - ☐ **b.** wonder
   - ☐ **c.** ask

4. Most Kaw legends were about "Good Woman," who led Kaw warriors into battle after battle.

   LEGENDS
   - ☐ **a.** pictures
   - ☐ **b.** stories
   - ☐ **c.** fights

5. Under the leadership of "Good Woman," the warriors were always victorious.

   VICTORIOUS
   - ☐ **a.** cautious
   - ☐ **b.** peaceful
   - ☐ **c.** triumphant

6. Mary and Roger went to separate "territories" and were not supposed to communicate with each other.

   COMMUNICATE
   - ☐ **a.** eat
   - ☐ **b.** work
   - ☐ **c.** talk

7. Grandfather demonstrated the way to eat a grasshopper.

   DEMONSTRATED
   - ☐ **a.** liked
   - ☐ **b.** learned
   - ☐ **c.** showed

8. Everyone said that for the next few days Mary and Roger would be dining on insects.

   DINING
   - ☐ **a.** catching
   - ☐ **b.** eating
   - ☐ **c.** worrying

9. Mary was unable to find a boat to sleep in. "There's not one boat here," she said dejectedly.

   DEJECTEDLY
   - ☐ **a.** cheerfully
   - ☐ **b.** sadly
   - ☐ **c.** hopefully

10. She suddenly realized that Ta-Na-E-Ka might be more fun than she had anticipated.

    ANTICIPATED
    - ☐ **a.** expected
    - ☐ **b.** wanted
    - ☐ **c.** needed

Exercise E ~ Understanding Characters and Plot

The following questions review the **characters** and **plot** in the story. Put
an **X** in the box next to the correct answer.

1. Who is the main character in "Ta-Na-E-Ka"?
   - ☐ **a.** Grandfather
   - ☐ **b.** Mary
   - ☐ **c.** Roger

2. Select the sentence that best characterizes Mary.
   - ☐ **a.** She was independent and resourceful.
   - ☐ **b.** She was quiet and shy.
   - ☐ **c.** She was unable to handle new situations effectively.

3. How did Mary change during the course of the story?
   - ☐ **a.** She became convinced that the customs of the Kaw were very silly.
   - ☐ **b.** She lost confidence in her ability to succeed.
   - ☐ **c.** She learned to appreciate Ta-Na-E-Ka and her people.

4. At the end of the story, Grandfather
   - ☐ **a.** refused to forgive Mary for staying at the restaurant.
   - ☐ **b.** punished Mary by making her do her Ta-Na-E-Ka over again.
   - ☐ **c.** recognized that Mary had the skills she needed to survive in
     today's world.

5. What happened first in the plot of "Ta-Na-E-Ka"?
   - ☐ **a.** Grandfather asked Mary what she ate during her Ta-Na-E-Ka.
   - ☐ **b.** Mary and Roger kissed their parents and went off to the woods.
   - ☐ **c.** Mary told Ernie about Ta-Na-E-Ka.

6. What happened last in the plot of the story?
   - ☐ **a.** Ernie gave Mary a bundle of clothes.
   - ☐ **b.** Mary borrowed five dollars from Mrs. Richardson.
   - ☐ **c.** Grandfather revealed that he ate the meat from a deer on his
     Ta-Na-E-Ka.

7. Which one of the following played the most important part in the plot of
   the story?
   - ☐ **a.** Mary overslept on the floor of Ernie's Riverside restaurant.
   - ☐ **b.** When Roger returned home, his feet were red and sore.
   - ☐ **c.** Mary played on the riverbank and watched the birds.

Exercise F ~ Vocabulary Review

Write a complete sentence for each word.

1. confided _____

_____

2. embraced _____

_____

3. hospitality _____

_____

4. nourishing _____

_____

5. participate _____

_____

6. survival _____

_____

7. nightmares _____

_____

8. heritage _____

_____

9. endurance _____

_____

10. legends _____

_____

STUDYING THE STORY

A. Looking Back at the Story

Discuss these questions with your partner or with the group. Your teacher may ask you to write your answer to one or more of the questions.

- For months, Mary had been thinking that Ta-Na-E-Ka was pretty silly. However, when Ernie said so, Mary immediately became angry and defended the custom. Why do you think Mary acted the way she did?

- In what ways was Mary's Ta-Na-E-Ka a valuable learning experience for both Mary and Grandfather?

- Do you think that Mary didn't "play by the rules" during her Ta-Na-E-Ka, or was she right to use any method available during her "test of survival"? Explain your reasoning.

- If you were Grandfather, would you have made Mary do her Ta-Na-E-Ka over? Give reasons to support your answer.

B. Using a Chart to Show How Characters Change

Sometimes characters change during the course of a story. When this occurs, it is called **character development**. On the chart below, list the changes in Mary and Grandfather during the story.

Changes in Mary and Grandfather	
Mary at Beginning of Story	**Mary at End of Story**
Grandfather at Beginning of Story	**Grandfather at End of Story**

THINKING ABOUT LITERATURE

1. Do you think that Ta-Na-E-Ka still serves a valuable purpose today, or do you believe that it has outlived its usefulness or may be too dangerous? On the following lines, write a **persuasive composition**. Explain why you think that the tradition of Ta-Na-E-Ka should (or should *not*) be continued. State your point of view in the **introductory paragraph**. Present your arguments in the **body** of the composition. State your point of view again in the **concluding paragraph**.

_____

_____

_____

_____

_____

_____

_____

_____

_____

_____

_____

_____

_____

_____

_____

2. Many families have certain customs or traditions. Describe a custom or tradition in your family or a family you know. Is it a tradition you think is likely to continue? Explain why.

_____

_____

_____

_____

_____

_____

3. Grandfather

a. Why is the speaker puzzled by his grandfather?

_____

_____

b. How can you explain the fact that Grandfather "sees" better and moves along the trail more easily than the much younger man?

_____

_____

c. Compare Grandfather on the trail and Grandfather at home.

_____

_____

_____

d. How is Grandfather in the poem similar to Grandfather in "Ta-Na-E-Ka"?

_____

_____

_____

_____

THE CIRCUIT

BY FRANCISCO JIMÉNEZ

GETTING READY TO READ

1. The Story and You

In this story, you will meet Panchito and his family. Since they continually travel in search of work, there is no place that they can really call "home." Tell about a time you moved from one place to another. Where did you move from? Where did you move to? Tell why you moved and how you felt about moving. Do you think it is likely that you will be moving again soon? Why? If you could choose any place to live, where would that be? Explain.

2. Learning About Literature

When an author writes a book about his or her life, the book is called an **autobiography**. Since "The Circuit" is based on events that the author experienced, it is an autobiographical story. When you read "The Circuit," you will probably find, as most readers do, that the story is completely believable and very "true to life."

3. Looking Ahead

Look at the illustration on the left. What clue in the picture suggests that the **setting** of the story is some years ago? How can you tell that the story deals with moving? Judging by the picture, who is the **main character** in the story? On the right side of the illustration, you can see someone putting grapes into a box. Does this provide a hint to what the story is about? Read on to see if you are right.

THE CIRCUIT

BY FRANCISCO JIMÉNEZ

They worked twelve hours a day, seven days a week . . .

It was that time of year again. Ito, the strawberry sharecropper,[1] did not smile. It was natural. The peak of the strawberry season was over and the last few days the workers, most of them braceros,[2] were not picking as many boxes as they had during the months of June and July.

As the last days of August disappeared, so did the number of braceros. Sunday, only one—the best picker—came to work. I liked him. Sometimes we talked during our half-hour lunch break. That is how I found out he was from Jalisco, the same state in Mexico my family was from. That Sunday was the last time I saw him.

When the sun had tired and sunk behind the mountains, Ito signaled us that it was time to go home. "*Ya esora,*"[3] he yelled in his broken Spanish. Those were the words I waited for twelve hours a day, every day, seven days a week, week after week. And the thought of not hearing them again saddened me.

As we drove home Papa did not say a word. With both hands on the wheel, he stared at the dirt road. My older brother, Roberto, was also silent. He leaned his head back and closed his eyes. Once in a while he cleared from his throat the dust that blew in from outside.

Yes, it was that time of year. When I opened the front door to the shack, I stopped. Everything we owned was neatly packed in cardboard boxes. Suddenly I felt even more the weight of hours, days, weeks, and months of work. I sat down on a box. The thought of having to move to Fresno and knowing what was in store for me there brought tears to my eyes.

---

1. *sharecropper*: someone who works on a farm in return for a share of the crops

2. *braceros*: Mexican farmworkers

3. *Ya esora*: It's time to go.

That night I could not sleep. I lay in bed thinking about how much I hated this move.

A little before five o'clock in the morning, Papa woke everyone up. A few minutes later, the yelling and screaming of my little brothers and sisters, for whom the move was a great adventure, broke the silence of dawn. Shortly, the barking of the dogs accompanied them.

While we packed the breakfast dishes, Papa went outside to start the "Carcanchita." That was the name Papa gave his old '38 black Plymouth. He bought it in a used-car lot in Santa Rosa in the winter of 1949. Papa was very proud of his car. "*Mi Carcanchita,*" my little jalopy, he called it. He had a right to be proud of it. He spent a lot of time looking at other cars before buying this one. When he finally chose the "Carcanchita," he checked it thoroughly before driving it out of the car lot. He examined every inch of the car. He listened to the motor, tilting his head from side to side like a parrot, trying to detect any noises that spelled car trouble. After being satisfied with the looks and sounds of the car, Papa then insisted on knowing who the original owner was. He never did find out from the car salesman. But he bought the car anyway. Papa figured the original owner must have been an important man because behind the rear seat of the car he found a blue necktie.

Papa parked the car out in front and left the motor running. *"Listo"* (ready), he yelled. Without saying a word, Roberto and I began to carry the boxes out to the car. Roberto carried the two big boxes and I carried the two smaller ones. Papa then threw the mattress on top of the car roof and tied it with ropes to the front and rear bumpers.

Everything was packed except Mama's pot. It was an old large galvanized pot[4] she had picked up at an army surplus store in Santa Maria the year I was born. The pot was full of dents and nicks, and

4. *galvanized pot*: a pot that has been coated with a material to keep it from rusting

the more dents and nicks it had, the more Mama liked it. *"Mi olla"* (my pot), she used to say proudly.

I held the front door open as Mama carefully carried out her pot by both handles, making sure not to spill the cooked beans. When she got to the car, Papa reached out to help her with it. Roberto opened the rear car door and Papa gently placed it on the floor behind the front seat. All of us then climbed in. Papa sighed, wiped the sweat off his forehead with his sleeve, and said wearily: *"Es todo"* (that's it).

As we drove away, I felt a lump in my throat. I turned around and looked at our little shack for the last time.

At sunset we drove into a labor camp near Fresno. Since Papa did not speak English, Mama asked the camp foreman if he needed any more workers. "We don't need no more," said the foreman, scratching his head. "Check with Sullivan down the road. Can't miss him. He lives in a big white house with a fence around it."

When we got there, Mama walked up to the house. She went through a white gate, past a row of rose bushes, up the stairs to the front door. She rang the doorbell. The porch light went on and a tall husky man came out. They exchanged a few words. After the man went in, Mama clasped her hands and hurried back to the car. "We have work! Mr. Sullivan said we can stay there the whole season," she said gasping and pointing to an old garage near the stables.

The garage was worn out by the years. It had no windows. The walls, eaten by termites, strained to support the roof full of holes. The loose dirt floor, populated by earthworms, looked like a gray road map.

That night, by the light of a kerosene lamp, we unpacked and cleaned our new home. Roberto swept away the loose dirt, leaving the hard ground. Papa plugged the holes in the walls with old newspapers and tin can tops. Mama fed my little brothers and sisters. Papa and Roberto then brought in the mattress and placed it on the far corner of the garage. "Mama, you and the little ones sleep on the mattress. Roberto, Panchito, and I will sleep outside under the trees," Papa said.

Early next morning Mr. Sullivan showed us where his crop was, and after breakfast, Papa, Roberto, and I headed for the vineyard to pick.

Around nine o'clock the temperature had risen to almost one hundred degrees. I was completely soaked in sweat and my mouth felt as if I had been chewing on a handkerchief. I walked over to the end of the row, picked up the jug of water we had brought, and began drinking. "Don't drink too much; you'll get sick," Roberto shouted. No sooner had he said that than I felt sick to my stomach. I dropped to my knees and let the jug roll off my hands. I remained motionless with my eyes glued on the hot sandy ground. All I could hear was the drone of insects. Slowly I began to recover. I poured water over my face and neck and watched the black mud run down my arms and hit the ground.

I still felt a little dizzy when we took a break to eat lunch. It was past two o'clock and we sat underneath a large walnut tree that was on the side of the road. While we ate, Papa jotted down the number of boxes we had picked. Roberto drew designs on the ground with a stick. Suddenly I noticed Papa's face turn pale as he looked down the road. "Here comes the school bus," he whispered loudly in alarm. Instinctively, Roberto and I ran and hid in the vineyards. We did not want to get in trouble for not going to school. The yellow bus stopped in front of Mr. Sullivan's house. Two neatly dressed boys about my age got off. They carried books under their arms. After they crossed the street, the bus drove away. Roberto and I came out from hiding and joined Papa. "*Tienen que tener cuidado*" (you have to be careful), he warned us.

After lunch we went back to work. The sun kept beating down. The buzzing insects, the wet sweat, and the hot dry dust made the afternoon seem to last forever. Finally the mountains around the valley reached out and swallowed the sun. Within an hour it was too dark to continue picking. The vines blanketed the grapes, making it difficult to see the bunches. "*Vámonos*,"[5] said Papa, signaling to us that it was time to quit work. Papa then took out a pencil and began to figure out how much we had earned our first day. He wrote down

---

5. *Vámonos*: Let's go.

numbers, crossed some out, wrote down some more. "*Quince*"
(fifteen dollars), he murmured.

When we arrived home, we took a cold shower underneath a
waterhose. We then sat down to eat dinner around some wooden
crates that served as a table. Mama had cooked a special meal for us.
We had rice and tortillas with *carne con chile*, my favorite dish.

The next morning I could hardly move. My body ached all over.
I felt little control over my arms and legs. This feeling went on every
morning for days until my muscles finally got used to the work.

It was Monday, the first week of November. The grape season was
over and I could now go to school. I woke up early that morning and
lay in bed, looking at the stars and savoring the thought of not going
to work and of starting sixth grade for the first time that year. Since I
could not sleep, I decided to get up and join Papa and Roberto at
breakfast. I sat at the table across from Roberto, but I kept my head
down. I did not want to look up and face him. I knew he was sad. He
was not going to school today. He was not going tomorrow, or next
week, or next month. He would not go until the cotton season was
over, and that was sometime in February. I rubbed my hands
together and watched the dry, acid-stained skin fall to the floor in
little rolls.

When Papa and Roberto left for work, I felt relief. I walked to the
top of a small grade next to the shack and watched the
"Carcanchita" disappear in the distance in a cloud of dust.

Two hours later, around eight o'clock, I stood by the side of the
road waiting for school bus number twenty. When it arrived I
climbed in. No one noticed me. Everyone was busy either talking or
yelling. I sat in an empty seat in the back.

When the bus stopped in front of the school, I felt very nervous.
I looked out the bus window and saw boys and girls carrying books
under their arms. I felt empty. I put my hands in my pants pockets
and walked to the principal's office. When I entered I heard a
woman's voice say: "May I help you?" I was startled. I had not heard
English for months. For a few seconds I remained speechless.
I looked at the lady who waited for an answer.

My first instinct was to answer her in Spanish, but I held back.
Finally, after struggling for English words I managed to tell her that I
wanted to enroll in the sixth grade. After answering many questions,
I was led to the classroom.

Mr. Lema, the sixth-grade teacher, greeted me and assigned me a desk. He then introduced me to the class. I was so nervous and scared at that moment when everyone's eyes were on me that I wished I were with Papa and Roberto picking cotton. After taking roll, Mr. Lema gave the class the assignment for the first hour. "The first thing we have to do this morning is finish reading the story we began yesterday," he said enthusiastically. He walked up to me, handed me an English book, and asked me to read. "We are on page 125," he said politely. When I heard this, I felt my blood rush to my head; I felt dizzy. "Would you like to read?" he asked hesitantly. I opened the book to page 125. My mouth was dry. My eyes began to water. I could not begin. "You can read later," Mr. Lema said understandingly.

For the rest of the reading period I kept getting angrier and angrier with myself. I should have read, I thought to myself.

During recess I went into the restroom and opened my English book to page 125. I began to read in a low voice, pretending I was in class. There were many words I did not know. I closed the book and headed back to the classroom.

Mr. Lema was sitting at his desk correcting papers. When I entered he looked up at me and smiled. I felt better. I walked up to him and asked if he could help me with the new words. "Gladly," he said.

The rest of the month I spent my lunch hours working on English with Mr. Lema, my best friend at school.

One Friday during lunch hour Mr. Lema asked me to take a walk with him to the music room. "Do you like music?" he asked me as we entered the building.

"Yes, I like Mexican *corridos*,"[6] I answered. He then picked up a trumpet, blew on it and handed it to me. The sound gave me goose bumps. I knew that sound. I had heard it in many Mexican corridos. "How would you like to learn how to play it?" he asked. He must have read my face because before I could answer, he added: "I'll teach you how to play it during our lunch hours."

That day I could hardly wait to get home to tell Papa and Mama the great news. As I got off the bus, my little brothers and sisters ran up to meet me. They were yelling and screaming. I thought they were happy to see me, but when I opened the door to our shack, I saw that everything we owned was neatly packed in cardboard boxes.

Read the last paragraph of the story again. What can you conclude, or figure out, has happened to Panchito's family? What is the family very likely to do now? When you **draw a conclusion**, you use information in the story to reach a decision.

Meet the Author

Francisco Jiménez was born in Jalisco, Mexico, and immigrated to California with his family when he was four years old. "The Circuit," based on the author's experiences growing up in California, was written in Spanish and then translated into English. When it was published in 1973, it won *The Arizona Quarterly* Annual Award. The author earned a doctorate from Columbia University in New York, and now teaches Spanish language and literature at the University of Santa Clara in California. He has written and edited many articles and short stories.

---

6. *corridos*: popular songs; ballads

CHECK YOUR READING

Put an **X** in the box next to the correct answer.

Reading Comprehension

1. At the beginning of the story, Panchito was sad because he
   - ☐ **a.** hadn't seen his family for a long time.
   - ☐ **b.** didn't want to move to Fresno.
   - ☐ **c.** was feeling ill.

2. How did Papa feel about his used car?
   - ☐ **a.** He was very proud of it.
   - ☐ **b.** He was ashamed of it.
   - ☐ **c.** He didn't care about it.

3. Mr. Sullivan said that the family could stay
   - ☐ **a.** in a big white house.
   - ☐ **b.** with some friends who lived nearby.
   - ☐ **c.** in a garage.

4. How much did the family earn the first day on the new job?
   - ☐ **a.** ten dollars
   - ☐ **b.** fifteen dollars
   - ☐ **c.** twenty dollars

5. Why didn't Panchito read to the class on his first day at school?
   - ☐ **a.** He was too nervous to read.
   - ☐ **b.** He didn't understand any of the words
   - ☐ **c.** He didn't have a book.

6. Mr. Lema said that he would teach Panchito how to play
   - ☐ **a.** the piano.
   - ☐ **b.** the trumpet.
   - ☐ **c.** the violin.

7. At the end of the story, Panchito discovered that
   - ☐ **a.** Mr. Lema had a new job.
   - ☐ **b.** the family had to leave in a month.
   - ☐ **c.** everything they owned was packed in boxes.

Vocabulary

8. He tried to detect if there was anything wrong with the car. The word *detect* means to
   - ☐ **a.** stop.
   - ☐ **b.** watch.
   - ☐ **c.** discover.

9. Papa asked, "Who was the original owner of the car?" The word *original* means
   - ☐ **a.** first.
   - ☐ **b.** last.
   - ☐ **c.** best.

Idioms

10. He knew what was in store for him in Fresno, so he wanted to stay home. The idiom *in store* means
    - ☐ **a.** in a grocery store.
    - ☐ **b.** in a shop.
    - ☐ **c.** in the future.

How many questions did you answer correctly? Circle your score. Then fill in your score on the Score Chart on page 184.

Number Correct	Score
1	10
2	20
3	30
4	40
5	50
6	60
7	70
8	80
9	90
10	100

UNDERSTANDING THE STORY

Exercise A ~ Checking Comprehension

Answer each question by writing a complete sentence. Be sure your sentences are grammatically correct. You may look back at the story.

1. Where was the family moving to at the beginning of "The Circuit"?

_____

2. What did Papa find behind a seat in the car before he bought it?

_____

3. How long did Mr. Sullivan say the family could stay?

_____

4. Where did the family live when they worked for Mr. Sullivan?

_____

5. Where did Roberto, Panchito, and Papa sleep?

_____

6. How much did the family earn their first day on the new job?

_____

7. Why was Panchito able to go to school in November?

_____

8. What grade was Panchito in at school?

_____

9. How did Panchito spend his lunch hour at school?

_____

10. At the end of the story, what did Panchito see when he opened the door?

_____

Exercise B ~ Adding Vocabulary

In the box are 10 words from the story. Complete each sentence by adding the correct word.

vineyard	pretending	populated	crates	peak
dawn	enroll	husky	muscles	instinct

1. Everyone got up at five o'clock in the morning, and the family was ready to leave by _____.

2. Since the _____ of the season was over, some of the workers had left.

3. Mama rang the bell and a tall, _____ man came to the door.

4. The ground was covered with earth, which was _____ by worms.

5. Papa, Roberto, and Panchito began to pick grapes in the

   _____.

6. Panchito ached all over until his _____ finally got used to the work.

7. They ate dinner on wooden _____ that served as a table.

8. When Panchito arrived at school, he explained that he wanted to

   _____ in the sixth grade.

9. Although Panchito's first _____ was to speak Spanish, he answered in English.

10. He read softly in the restroom, _____ that he was in class.

Exercise C ~ Combining Sentences

Part A

Combine two **simple sentences** into one **complex sentence** by using the **subordinating conjunction** in parentheses. Begin the sentence with the conjunction, and use a comma at the end of the clause. Write the complex sentence on the line. The first one has been done for you.

Common Subordinating Conjunctions

after	since	although	though
when	as	if	while

1. The strawberry season was over. The family had to move. (since)

   Since the strawberry season was over, the family
   had to move.

2. The car was very old. Papa liked it very much. (although)

   _____

   _____

3. Papa packed the car. Mama prepared food for the trip. (while)

   _____

   _____

4. The family drove away. Panchito looked back at their little shack. (as)

   _____

   _____

5. The work was very hard. Panchito got used to it. (though)

   _____

   _____

6. Panchito entered the classroom. Mr. Lema introduced him to the class. (after)

   _____

   _____

7. You can come here during your lunch hour. I will help you with your English. (if)

_____

_____

8. Panchito studied every day. His English improved rapidly. (since)

_____

_____

9. Panchito opened the door. He saw the boxes on the floor. (when)

_____

_____

Part B
Combine two **simple sentences** into one **complex sentence** by using the **subordinating conjunctions** below. Begin the sentence with the conjunction, and use a comma at the end of the clause. Write the complex sentence on the line. Use each conjunction once.

after	although	since	while

1. Papa didn't speak English. Mama spoke to Mr. Sullivan.

_____

_____

2. Roberto swept the floor. Papa fixed the walls.

_____

3. Roberto wanted to go to school now. He had to wait until February.

_____

_____

4. Panchito drank too much water. He felt sick.

_____

Exercise D ~ Finding Synonyms

Read the sentence. Then select the **synonym** (the word most similar in meaning) for the word in capital letters. Put an **X** in the box next to the correct answer. Each capitalized word appears in the story.

1. Papa checked the car thoroughly before driving it out of the lot.

   THOROUGHLY
   - ☐ **a.** quickly
   - ☐ **b.** carefully
   - ☐ **c.** quietly

2. He listened to the motor, tilting his head from side to side.

   TILTING
   - ☐ **a.** leaning
   - ☐ **b.** hearing
   - ☐ **c.** keeping

3. Panchito lay in bed looking at the stars and savoring the thought of not going to work.

   SAVORING
   - ☐ **a.** watching
   - ☐ **b.** hating
   - ☐ **c.** enjoying

4. Papa plugged the holes in the walls with old newspapers.

   PLUGGED
   - ☐ **a.** emptied
   - ☐ **b.** filled
   - ☐ **c.** broke

5. The only thing that Panchito could hear was the drone of insects.

   DRONE
   - ☐ **a.** humming
   - ☐ **b.** work
   - ☐ **c.** wings

6. His father took a pencil and jotted down the number of boxes they had filled.

   JOTTED
   - ☐ **a.** carried
   - ☐ **b.** wrote
   - ☐ **c.** read

7. He had not heard English for so long, he was startled when she said, "May I help you?"

   STARTLED
   - ☐ **a.** confused
   - ☐ **b.** bothered
   - ☐ **c.** surprised

8. She waited for him to answer, but he was speechless.

   SPEECHLESS
   - ☐ **a.** silent
   - ☐ **b.** lost
   - ☐ **c.** pleased

9. The teacher, Mr. Lema, greeted Panchito and assigned him a seat.

   ASSIGNED
   - ☐ **a.** gave
   - ☐ **b.** needed
   - ☐ **c.** demanded

10. "You're sure to enjoy the story we began reading yesterday," he said enthusiastically.

    ENTHUSIASTICALLY
    - ☐ **a.** shyly
    - ☐ **b.** angrily
    - ☐ **c.** eagerly

Exercise E ~ Thinking Critically

How well did you "read between the lines"? The following questions will help you read critically. Put an **X** in the box next to the correct answer.

1. The last sentence of "The Circuit" suggests that
   - ☐ **a.** the shack was too small for the family.
   - ☐ **b.** the family owned many things.
   - ☐ **c.** the family was about to move again.

2. When Panchito saw the boxes at the end of the story, he probably felt
   - ☐ **a.** pleased.
   - ☐ **b.** shocked and sad.
   - ☐ **c.** quite calm.

3. Which statement is true?
   - ☐ **a.** The family worked hard and long for very little money.
   - ☐ **b.** The family did not work very hard.
   - ☐ **c.** The family usually worked in the same place all year.

4. The story shows how much Panchito valued
   - ☐ **a.** new cars.
   - ☐ **b.** fancy clothing.
   - ☐ **c.** education.

5. "The Circuit" is a true story. We may infer that the author was
   - ☐ **a.** Papa.
   - ☐ **b.** Mama.
   - ☐ **c.** Panchito.

Exercise F ~ **Vocabulary Review**

Write a complete sentence for each word.

1. detect _____

_____

2. original _____

_____

3. enroll _____

_____

4. husky _____

_____

5. populated _____

_____

6. crates _____

_____

7. savoring _____

_____

8. dawn _____

_____

9. instinct _____

_____

10. pretending _____

_____

STUDYING THE STORY

A. Looking Back at the Story

Discuss these questions with your partner or with the group. Your teacher may ask you to write you answer to one or more of the questions.

■ Why was it necessary for the family to move from place to place? What were some of the hardships the family had to endure? What strengths and qualities did the family possess that helped them deal with the difficulties they encountered?

■ Point out the various ways in which Mr. Lema helped Panchito and tried to make him feel more comfortable at school. How do you know that Panchito was a very enthusiastic student?

■ At the end of the story, Panchito rushed home to tell his family "the great news." However, when he opened the door, he saw that everything they owned was neatly packed in cardboard boxes. Explain how this incident makes the conclusion of the story sadder and more powerful.

B. Charting Events in the Correct Order

"The Circuit" is based on events that actually took place. Use the chart to put the events in the order in which they occurred. Write the correct letter in the box. Two letters have been done for you. You may look back at the story.

1 *d* ⇒ **2** ⇒ **3** ⇒ **4** *c* ⇒ **5** ⇒

6 ⇒ **7** ⇒ **8** ⇒ **9** ⇒ **10**

a. Mama asked Mr. Sullivan if he had work for them to do.

b. Papa, Roberto, and Panchito picked grapes in the vineyard.

c. Mr. Sullivan told Mama that the family could stay for the season.

d. Ito told the family it was time to go home.

e. Panchito took a bus to his new school.

f. Mr. Lema said he would teach Panchito how to play the trumpet.

g. Papa drove the family to Fresno.

h. When Panchito opened the door, he saw everything was packed in cardboard boxes.

i. Mr. Lema greeted Panchito and assigned him a desk.

j. That night the family unpacked, and then they cleaned their new home.

THINKING ABOUT LITERATURE

1. As you know, "The Circuit" is an **autobiographical story**. This means it is based on events that took place in the author's life. Mr. Lema was actually the author's teacher, one of three teachers who changed the course of Mr. Jiménez's life.

Suppose that years after leaving Fresno, Panchito decided to write a letter to Mr. Lema. What do you think Panchito might say? On the lines below, write Panchito's letter. You will probably want to refer to Panchitos's first day at school and to the strong influence that Mr. Lema had on him. Add a date to your letter.

_____

(date)

Dear Mr. Lema,

_____

_____

_____

_____

_____

_____

_____

_____

_____

_____

Your friend,
Panchito

2. The word *circuit* may be defined as "a route or path that a person or persons follow regularly or repeatedly." Explain why "The Circuit" is such an appropriate title for the story. Give at least two reasons.

_____

_____

_____

_____

_____

_____

3. On the line below, write another title for the story that would also be appropriate. Put the title in quotation marks.

_____

4. When Panchito arrived at the school, his first instinct was to speak Spanish. However, he "held back" and struggled in English. Have you ever experienced a time when you felt your English was weak, but you "struggled through"? Tell what happened. If you prefer, describe how your English has improved over time. Give some examples.

_____

_____

_____

_____

_____

_____

_____

_____

_____

A SECRET FOR TWO

BY QUENTIN REYNOLDS

GETTING READY TO READ

1. The Story and You

In this story, you will meet Pierre and his horse, Joseph. As you will discover, they are a remarkable team. Many people consider animals to be loving and devoted companions. Why do you think this is so? Has a dog, cat, or other animal been very meaningful to you or to someone you know? If so, explain why.

2. Learning About Literature

You know that the plot tells the important incidents or events that take place in a story. The **theme** of a story is different from the plot. The theme is the main idea of the story. Ask yourself, "What is the main point, or the main idea, the author is making?" That is the theme. Try to find the theme of "A Secret for Two."

3. Looking Ahead

Look at the illustration on the left. Judging by the picture, what do you think the story is about? How do you think the main character earns a living? Why? When do you think the story takes place? The story is called "A Secret for Two." What do you think the secret might be? Read on to see if you are right.

A Secret for Two

by Quentin Reynolds

Is it really possible to keep a secret?

Montreal[1] is a very large city but, like all large cities, it has some very small streets. Streets, for instance, like Prince Edward Street, which is only four blocks long, ending in a cul-de-sac.[2] No one knew Prince Edward as well as did Pierre Dupin, for Pierre had delivered milk to the families on the street for 30 years now.

During the past 15 years, the horse that drew the milk wagon used by Pierre was a large white horse named Joseph. In Montreal, especially in that part of Montreal that is very French, the animals, like children, are often given the names of saints. When the big white horse first came to the Provinçale Milk Company, he didn't have a name. They told Pierre that he could use the white horse henceforth. Pierre stroked the softness of the horse's neck, he stroked the sheen of its splendid belly, and he looked in the eyes of the horse.

"That is a kind horse, a gentle and a faithful horse," Pierre said, "and I can see a beautiful spirit shining out of the eyes of this horse. I will name him after good St. Joseph, who was also kind and gentle and faithful and had a beautiful spirit."

Within a year, Joseph knew the milk route as well as Pierre. Pierre used to boast that he didn't need reins—he never touched them. Each morning, Pierre arrived at the stables of the Provinçale Milk Company at five o'clock. The wagon would be loaded and Joseph hitched to it. Pierre would call, *"Bon jour, vieil ami,"*[3] as he climbed into his seat and Joseph would turn his head and the other drivers would smile and say that the horse would smile at Pierre. Then Jacques, the foreman, would say, "All right, Pierre, go on," and Pierre

---

1. *Montreal:* a city in Canada

2. *cul-de-sac:* a dead-end street; a street with only one opening

3. *Bonjour, vieil ami:* the French words for "Hello, old friend."

would call softly to Joseph, *"Avance, mon ami,"*[4] and this splendid combination would stalk proudly down the street.

The wagon, without any direction from Pierre, would roll three blocks down St. Catherine Street; then turn right two blocks along Roslyn Avenue; then left, for that was Prince Edward Street. The horse would stop at the first house, allow Pierre perhaps 30 seconds to get down from his seat and put a bottle of milk at the front door and would then go on, skipping two houses and stopping at the third. And so they went, down the street. Then Joseph, still without any direction from Pierre, would turn around and come back along the other side. Yes, Joseph was a smart horse.

Pierre would boast at the stable of Joseph's skill. "I never touch the reins. He knows just where to stop. Why, a blind man could handle my route with Joseph pulling the wagon."

So it went for many years—always the same. Pierre and Joseph both grew old together, but gradually, not suddenly. Pierre's huge walrus mustache was pure white now, and Joseph didn't lift his knees so high or raise his head quite as much. Jacques, the foreman of the stables, never noticed that they were both getting old until Pierre appeared one day carrying a heavy walking stick.

"Hey, Pierre," Jacques laughed. "Maybe you got the gout,[5] hey?"

"Mais, oui,[6] Jacques," Pierre said uncertainly. "One grows old. One's legs get tired."

"You should teach the horse to carry the milk to the front door

---

4. *Avance, mon ami:* the French words for "Go ahead, my friend."

5. *gout:* a disease that often affects the feet

6. *Mais oui:* the French words for "Oh, yes"

for you," Jacques told him. "He does everything else."

Pierre knew every one of the 40 families he served on Prince Edward Street. The cooks knew that Pierre could neither read nor write, so instead of following the usual custom of leaving a note in an empty bottle if an additional quart of milk was needed they would sing out when they heard the rumble of his wagon wheels over the cobbled[7] street, "Bring an extra quart this morning, Pierre."

Pierre had a remarkable memory. When he arrived at the stable, he'd always remember to tell Jacques, "The Parquins took an extra quart this morning; the Lemoines bought a pint of cream."

Jacques would note these things in a little book he always carried. Most of the drivers had to make out the weekly bills and collect the money, but Jacques, liking Pierre, had always excused him from this task. All Pierre had to do was to arrive at five in the morning, walk to his wagon, which was always in the same spot at the curb, and deliver his milk. He returned some two hours later, got stiffly from his seat, called a cheery "*Au 'voir*"[8] to Jacques, and then limped slowly down the street.

One morning, the president of Provinçale Milk Company came to inspect the early morning deliveries. Jacques pointed Pierre out to him and said, "Watch how he talks to that horse. See how the horse listens and how he turns his head toward Pierre? See the look in that horse's eyes? You know, I think those two share a secret. I have often noticed it. It is as though they both sometimes chuckle at us as they go off on their route. Pierre is a good man, Monsieur[9] President, but he gets old. Would it be too bold for me to suggest that he be retired and be given perhaps a small pension?" he added anxiously.

"But of course," the president laughed. "I know his record. He has been on this route now for thirty years and never once has there been a complaint. Tell him it is time he rested. His salary will go on just the same."

But Pierre refused to retire. He was panic-stricken at the thought of not driving Joseph every day. "We are two old men," he said to Jacques. "Let us wear out together. When Joseph is ready to retire— then I, too, will quit."

---

7. *cobbled:* As used here, the word means "a street paved with cobblestones—wide, heavy stones."

8. *Au'voir:* the French word for "Good-bye"

9. *Monsieur:* the French word for "Mister"

Jacques, who was a kind man, understood. There was something about Pierre and Joseph that made a man smile tenderly. It was as though each drew some hidden strength from the other. When Pierre was sitting in his seat, and when Joseph was hitched to the wagon, neither seemed old. But when they finished their work, then Pierre would limp down the street slowly, seeming very old indeed, and the horse's head would drop and he would walk very wearily to his stall.

Then one morning, Jacques had dreadful news for Pierre when he arrived. It was a cold morning and still pitch-dark. The air was like iced wine that morning and the snow, which had fallen during the night, glistened like a million diamonds piled together.

Jacques said, "Pierre, your horse, Joseph, did not wake this morning. He was very old, Pierre, he was twenty-five, and that is like seventy-five for a man."

"Yes," Pierre said slowly. "Yes. I am seventy-five. And I cannot see Joseph again."

"Of course you can," Jacques soothed. "He is over in his stall, looking very peaceful. Go over and see him."

Pierre took one step forward, then turned. "No . . . no . . . you don't understand, Jacques."

Jacques clamped him on the shoulder. "We'll find another horse just as good as Joseph. Why, in a month you'll teach him to know your route as well as Joseph did. We'll—"

The look in Pierre's eyes stopped him. For years, Pierre had worn a heavy cap, the peak of which came low over his eyes, keeping the bitter morning wind out of them. Now Jacques looked into Pierre's eyes and he saw something that startled him. He saw a dead, lifeless look in them. The eyes were mirroring a grief that was in Pierre's heart and his soul. It was as though his heart and soul had died.

"Take today off, Pierre," Jacques said, but already Pierre was hobbling off down the street, and had one been near one would have seen tears streaming down his cheeks and have heard half-smothered sobs. Pierre walked to the corner and stepped into the street. There was a warning yell from the driver of a huge truck that was coming fast and there was the scream of brakes, but Pierre apparently heard neither.

Five minutes later, an ambulance driver said, "He's dead. Was killed instantly."

"I couldn't help it," the driver of the truck protested, "he walked right into my truck. He never saw it, I guess. Why, he walked into it as though he was blind."

The ambulance doctor bent down. "Blind? Of course the man was blind. See those cataracts?[10] This man has been blind for five years." He turned to Jacques. "You say he worked for you? Didn't you know he was blind?"

"No . . . no . . ." Jacques said softly. "None of us knew. Only one knew—a friend of his named Joseph. . . . It was a secret, I think, just between those two."

Meet the Author

Quentin Reynolds (1902-1965) was born in the Bronx, New York, and later attended Brown University. There he was an outstanding athlete, who starred in football, boxing, and swimming. Although Reynolds received a degree in law, he decided to pursue a career in journalism. For many years he was a leading war correspondent. Reynolds wrote two motion pictures, an autobiography, dozens of books, and hundreds of stories and articles. "A Secret for Two" is his best-known short story.

---

10. *cataracts:* a disease of the eye

Moco Limping

by David Nava Monreal

My dog hobbles[1]
with a stick
of a leg that
he drags behind
5 him as he moves.
And I was a man
that wanted a
beautiful, noble
animal as a pet.
10 I wanted him
to be strong and
capture all the
attention by
the savage grace
15 of his gait.[2]
I wanted him to
be the first
dog howling in
the pack.
20 The leader,
the brutal hunter
that broke through
the woods with
thunder.
25 But, instead he's
this rickety[3]

little canine[4]
that leaves trails
in the dirt
30 with his club foot.[5]
He's the stumbler
that trips while
chasing lethargic[6]
bees and butterflies.
35 It hurts me to
see him so
abnormal,
so clumsy and
stupid.
40 My vain heart weeps
knowing he
is mine.
But then he turns
my way and
45 looks at me with
eyes that cry out
with life.
He jumps at me with
his feeble paws.
50 I feel his warm fur
and his imperfection[7] is
forgotten.

---

1. *hobbles*: walks in an unusual way; walks with a limp

2. *gait*: way of walking

3. *rickety*: weak and shaky

4. *canine*: dog

5. *club foot*: a foot that has not grown correctly. It is usually short and may have an unusual shape

6. *lethargic*: slow moving; lazy

7. *imperfection*: As used here, the word means "fault."

CHECK YOUR READING

Put an **X** in the box next to the correct answer.

Reading Comprehension

1. Prince Edward Street is
- ☐ **a.** a very wide avenue.
- ☐ **b.** in a small town.
- ☐ **c.** four blocks long.

2. Pierre worked for the milk company for
- ☐ **a.** nearly ten years.
- ☐ **b.** exactly fifteen years.
- ☐ **c.** thirty years.

3. According to Pierre, his horse was
- ☐ **a.** kind, gentle, and faithful.
- ☐ **b.** not particularly helpful.
- ☐ **c.** a great deal of trouble.

4. Pierre knew what his customers wanted because they
- ☐ **a.** left notes in an empty bottle.
- ☐ **b.** called out their orders.
- ☐ **c.** sent letters to the company.

5. Jacques excused Pierre from the task of
- ☐ **a.** making out the monthly bills.
- ☐ **b.** delivering large orders.
- ☐ **c.** starting out early in the morning.

6. Pierre received the dreadful news that
- ☐ **a.** he had been fired.
- ☐ **b.** Joseph had died.
- ☐ **c.** the company was going out of business.

7. At the end of the story, the reader learns that Pierre
- ☐ **a.** hated his job.
- ☐ **b.** was blind.
- ☐ **c.** was going to receive a raise in salary.

Vocabulary

8. They gave Pierre a white horse, which Pierre used henceforth. The word *henceforth* means
- ☐ **a.** from that time on.
- ☐ **b.** day and night.
- ☐ **c.** occasionally.

9. There was a cry from the driver and the scream of brakes, but Pierre apparently heard nothing. The word *apparently* means
- ☐ **a.** cautiously.
- ☐ **b.** foolishly.
- ☐ **c.** seemingly.

Idioms

10. Pierre and his horse began to wear out together. As used here, the idiom *wear out* means
- ☐ **a.** tire out.
- ☐ **b.** stay out.
- ☐ **c.** help out.

UNDERSTANDING THE STORY

Exercise A ~ Checking Comprehension

Answer each question with a complete sentence. Be sure your sentences are grammatically correct. You may look back at the story.

1. How long had Pierre delivered milk to the families on the street?

_____

2. Who did Pierre name the horse after?

_____

3. What time did Pierre arrive at the stables of the milk company every morning?

_____

4. When did Jacques notice that Pierre was getting old?

_____

5. How many families did Pierre serve on Prince Edward Street?

_____

6. What had Pierre worn for years?

_____

7. When did Pierre plan to quit?

_____

8. What did Jacques see when he looked into Pierre's eyes?

_____

9. How did Pierre die?

_____

_____

10. What did the doctor reveal about Pierre?

_____

Exercise B ~ Adding Vocabulary

In the box are 8 words from the story. Complete each sentence by adding the
correct word. Use each word once.

complaint	combination	moustache	pension
ambulance	pint	streaming	retire

1. For fifteen years, Pierre and Joseph were a proud

_____ on Prince Edward Street.

2. Sometimes, customers asked for an extra quart of milk or a

_____ of cream.

3. As long as Joseph was willing to work, Pierre refused to

_____.

4. In all the years that Pierre had worked on his route, no customer had

ever made a _____ about him.

5. When he grew old, Pierre's _____ became pure
white.

6. The president of the company offered Pierre a

_____ for his many years of excellent service.

7. Pierre was sobbing with grief, and tears were _____
down his cheeks.

8. The driver of the _____ said that Pierre was dead.

Exercise C ~ Direct Quotations and Reported Speech

Change the direct quotations to reported speech by using the word *if*. Make the necessary changes in tense and pronouns. Write the new sentences on the lines. The first one has been done for you.

1. Pierre asked, "Can I have the white horse?"

Pierre asked if he could have the white horse.

2. Jacques asked Pierre, "Are you happy with Joseph?"

_____

3. Jacques wondered, "Are you sick, Pierre?"

_____

4. She asked, "May I have four quarts of milk?"

_____

5. Pierre asked her, "Are you having company?"

_____

6. The foreman asked, "Is Pierre too old to work?"

_____

7. The president wondered, "Will Pierre be willing to retire?"

_____

8. The doctor asked Jacques, "Did you know Pierre was blind?"

_____

Exercise D ~ Finding Synonyms

Read the sentence. Then select the **synonym** (the word most similar in meaning) for the word in capital letters. Put an **X** in the box next to the correct answer. Each capitalized word appears in the story.

1. Pierre knew immediately that he had selected a splendid horse.

   SPLENDID
   - ☐ **a.** lazy
   - ☐ **b.** interesting
   - ☐ **c.** marvelous

2. The president of the company came to inspect the early morning deliveries.

   INSPECT
   - ☐ **a.** examine
   - ☐ **b.** pack
   - ☐ **c.** sell

3. The foreman told the president, "Pierre is a good man."

   FOREMAN
   - ☐ **a.** friend
   - ☐ **b.** manager
   - ☐ **c.** relative

4. Occasionally, customers ordered an additional quart of milk.

   ADDITIONAL
   - ☐ **a.** expensive
   - ☐ **b.** different
   - ☐ **c.** extra

5. Pierre had a remarkable memory; he remembered everything.

   REMARKABLE
   - ☐ **a.** amazing
   - ☐ **b.** ordinary
   - ☐ **c.** poor

6. Pierre surely did not wish to stop working; he was panic-stricken at the thought of not driving Joseph.

   PANIC-STRICKEN
   - ☐ **a.** terrified
   - ☐ **b.** tempted
   - ☐ **c.** delighted

7. "You can see Joseph looking very peaceful in his stall," soothed Jacques.

   SOOTHED
   - ☐ **a.** warned
   - ☐ **b.** calmed
   - ☐ **c.** annoyed

8. After Joseph died, Pierre was seen hobbling sadly down the street.

   HOBBLING
   - ☐ **a.** crawling
   - ☐ **b.** limping
   - ☐ **c.** running

Exercise E ~ Understanding the Setting of a Story

As you know, the **setting** of a story is *where* and *when* the main action takes place. The setting plays a very important part in "A Secret for Two." How well did you understand the setting of the story? Put an **X** in the box next to the correct answer.

1. Where is the story set?
   - ☐ **a.** in Paris
   - ☐ **b.** in Montreal
   - ☐ **c.** in New York City

2. The fact that Pierre delivered milk with a horse and wagon suggests that the story takes place
   - ☐ **a.** in the past.
   - ☐ **b.** at the present time.
   - ☐ **c.** in the future.

3. It is fair to say that the setting of the story is actually limited to
   - ☐ **a.** an entire city.
   - ☐ **b.** a few miles.
   - ☐ **c.** several blocks.

4. Which one of the following facts is most important in "A Secret for Two"?
   - ☐ **a.** Pierre knew every one of the families he served on Prince Edward Street.
   - ☐ **b.** As Joseph grew older, he didn't raise his head quite as high.
   - ☐ **c.** Pierre named Joseph after a saint.

5. The story opens with a discussion of streets and concludes with
   - ☐ **a.** a conversation between Jacques and the company's president.
   - ☐ **b.** a description of the tasks that Pierre did daily.
   - ☐ **c.** the main character's death on a street.

Exercise F ~ **Vocabulary Review**

Write a complete sentence for each word or idiom.

1. complaint _____

_____

2. apparently _____

_____

3. combination _____

_____

4. pension _____

_____

5. moustache _____

_____

6. splendid _____

_____

7. retire _____

_____

8. inspect _____

_____

9. streaming _____

_____

10. wear out (idiom) _____

_____

STUDYING THE STORY

A. Looking Back at the Story

Discuss these questions with your partner or with the group. Your teacher may ask you to write your answer to one or more of the questions.

- What is the secret referred to in the title? Explain the ways in which Joseph assisted Pierre in fulfilling his responsibilities.

- Since Pierre was unable to read or write, how did he manage to accept orders and record his accounts? Point out, too, how Jacques helped Pierre.

- Do you think it was a coincidence that Pierre died at the age of seventy-five—the same age as Joseph who was "like . . . seventy-five for a man"? Explain.

- After Joseph died, when Jacques looked into Pierre's eyes, Jacques saw "a dead, lifeless look in them. The eyes were mirroring [Pierre's] grief." How do you think Pierre's grief contributed to his death?

B. Completing a Story Map

Suppose that you wanted to tell someone the story of "A Secret for Two." It would be helpful to organize your thoughts by using a story map. Complete the story map below.

A Secret for Two

Setting

Characters

Plot (important events that take place in the story):

1. _____
2. _____
3. _____
4. _____
5. _____
6. _____
7. _____
8. _____

THINKING ABOUT LITERATURE

1. The story map you completed can help you summarize the plot of "A Secret for Two." However, were you able to find the **theme**, or main idea, of the story? You were correct if you said that the theme is that two dear, old friends help each other and share a surprising secret (or something similar). At the conclusion of the story, the doctor asked Jacques, "Didn't you know he was blind? Jacques answered, "None of us knew . . . . It was a secret, I think, just between the two." Look back at the story. See if you can find two clues to the secret that Pierre was blind. One relates to the cap that Pierre wore. The other relates to what Jacques saw when he looked into Pierre's eyes. Write the clues below.

   a. _____

   b. _____

2. In literature, **foreshadowing** refers to clues or hints that suggest what will happen later in the story. Answer the following questions to see how well you understand foreshadowing.

   1. Which one of the following statements is an example of foreshadowing?
      - [ ] **a.** Pierre said, "I can see a beautiful spirit shining out of the eyes of the horse."
      - [ ] **b.** Pierre boasted, "Why a blind man could handle my route with Joseph pulling the wagon."
      - [ ] **c.** Jacques asked the president, "Would it be too bold of me to suggest that he be retired?"

   2. Which of the following statements is another example of foreshadowing?
      - [ ] **a.** Jacques said, "Pierre, your horse Joseph, did not wake up this morning."
      - [ ] **b.** "Take today off, Pierre," Jacques said.
      - [ ] **c.** Pierre said, slowly, "Yes. I am seventy-five. And I cannot see Joseph again."

   3. The fact that Pierre can no longer see very well is suggested when he
      - [ ] **a.** begins to use a heavy walking stick.
      - [ ] **b.** starts to complain about the job.
      - [ ] **c.** no longer works as capably as he previously did.

4. Which of the following foreshadows that the lives of Joseph and Pierre will end at about the same time?

☐ **a.** "I couldn't help it," the driver of the truck protested, "he walked right into my truck."

☐ **b.** "You should teach that horse to carry the milk to the front door for you," Jacques told him. "He does everything else."

☐ **c.** "We are two old men," he [Pierre] said to Jacques. "Let us wear out together. When Joseph is ready to retire—then I, too, will quit."

3. Moco Limping

a. What kind of dog does the speaker want? Why is the speaker disappointed in his dog? What makes the speaker forget about his dog's "imperfection"?

_____

_____

_____

b. What expressions in the poem strike you as particularly moving or powerful?

_____

_____

_____

c. In what ways is Moco similar to Joseph? How are they different?

_____

_____

_____

d. Why do you think "Moco Limping" appears in a unit with "A Secret for Two"? Write your answer below.

_____

_____

_____

_____

SCORE CHART

This is the Score Chart for **CHECK YOUR READING**. Shade in your score for each story. For example, if your score was 80 for **The Teacher**, look at the bottom of the chart for **The Teacher**. Then shade in the bar up to 80. By looking at this chart, you can see how well you did on each story.